CW00972046

PEOPLE NEED STILLNESS

A teenager said: 'I want it: it's like being at the eye of the hurricane.'
A businessman said: 'It gets me going on my way with a smooth mind.'
Isaiah said: 'Look to the rock from which you were hewn.'

PEOPLE NEED STILLNESS

Wanda Nash

DARTON · LONGMAN + TODD

First published in 1992 by
Darton, Longman and Todd Ltd
1 Spencer Court
140-142 Wandsworth High Street
London SW18 4JJ

Reprinted 1994

© 1992 Wanda Nash

ISBN 0–232–51971–4

A catalogue record for this book is available from the British Library

Phototypeset by Intype, London
Printed and bound in Great Britain
by BPCC Wheatons Ltd

To the late Bishop John Hare, who validated my need; to Molly, who was there when I launched out; and to all those many hundreds of ordinary people who have explored with me, looking for the rock from which we were hewn.

Acknowledgements

May I acknowledge my grateful thanks to:
Lord Coggan,
Father Michael Hollings,
Professor Harold Guite,
Brigid Pailthorpe, and
Jean Waddell,

for their patient encouragement throughout the gestation of this book. I hope the final version will meet with their expectations.

The illustrations in Part 1 and some of those in Part 2 are by Ken Smith: the remainder are by Tana Rivière.

CONTENTS

Part Three: FOLLOWING THROUGH

INTRODUCTION

The audience was sitting quietly impressed.

Then a dissenter burst out – 'It's all very well,' he said, 'all this talk about still centres. That's O.K. at the edge, where life is restful. But I want it *now*, in the middle of the racket, *here!* What about that?'

And so this book was born.

It will be about our longing to regain the stillness, the assuredness, the connectedness, which we risked losing when we were born, when the cord to the source of our living was cut. It's all about how we can tap into that centredness even when we are living at full stretch, when we are doing, striving, working, and about to break up because we are trying too hard.

In books about personal well-being or spirituality there are plenty of references to the need for a still centre, a well for replenishment and refilling; and there also seems to be plenty of material available for those who already 'meditate' — whichever brand of silence they prefer. But there is a gap between the two, between the aim and the goal as it were, a need for a 'how-to-do-it' manual, with explanations and suggestions about turning the need into an everyday practicality.

That is the gap this book sets out to fill. I like to think of it as a toolkit, a workmanlike bag containing basic ground plans, descriptions of different tools, ideas on approaching the work, and ways of using the various instruments. There are also some tools themselves. It is a book of how to get there, who to go with, what to do on arrival, and what sort of results to expect. It has been specifically designed to lie open, so that any page (but particularly those pages with examples of 'tools') can rest flat in front of the user, or in the centre of a group, to act as a focus.

There is so much to be busy about in today's world. In order to justify any time spent being still, we have to look at the question of the 'usefulness' of *being*, rather than *doing*. In the present climate of performance indicators and measurements of output, things to do with the spirit tend to be left out. This may be in spite of the fact that the values that drive us are fundamental to all our decisions. Our living standards, our attitudes to other people, our daily priorities, our powers of coping with frustration and pressure and anger, are all based on how much our striving is balanced by our grounding. We have a general hesitancy to speak of these very deeply rooted things. Discussion of them is hampered because they come from a place which, however real it is, is basically a place of no words. None the less more and more people of all ages and occupations are speaking of a hunger they feel, a need to explore this place.

A conscious interest in this place and how to get there is not limited to people with one set of convictions. It is an interest which expresses something that is common to all the great religions and philosophies of the world, though each system of belief may place particular emphases differently. This book includes ideas and techniques that are usable by anyone, whatever their allegiances, though no doubt each reader will want to be aware of differences between them that are crucial.

Some may go in to find a greater self-knowledge and recognition of who they really are.

Some may go in to find a mental state they need – peace, calm, contentment, equilibrium.
Some may go in in the company of Christ, and experience an increased awareness of the Holy Trinity.

But the book is not primarily about beliefs, nor is it concerned with comparing beliefs. It is about making spaces for the Spirit, for the Spirit to expand, in the conviction that the Spirit will place the name that s/he wills to be there. As a very famous (even notorious) public figure once said:

> What is born of the Spirit is spirit. The wind blows wherever it pleases, you hear its sound but you have no idea where it comes from and where it goes: that is how it is with all who are born of the Spirit.[1]

It is worth giving some thought to the fact that the word used in this passage can be translated with equal truth as 'wind', 'breath', 'spirit' and 'Spirit'. Is it a good idea to break it up into labelled confines?

The group was sitting round in a circle, each one rather intensely feeling the burdens of the others. One had spoken of the anger and frustration she felt in her dealings with a daunting boss; a father who was coping single-handed had talked of his practical bewilderment; another had said he felt he was hemmed in and pinned down by petty office routines, which cramped all his initiative and creativity; a young mother voiced her frustration at the unending demands and noise of bringing up three pre-school children. Others had spoken of broken relationships, confused values, financial alarms.

We all felt as though we were victims, and we were conscious of our inadequacy to cope with what we had found.

Then the group leader told us to sit with our eyes closed, and try to recall a real incident in our past lives when we had felt really alive, glad to have been born, at 'one' with ourselves. This we did.

The minutes passed . . .

Slowly each person began to connect with something and somewhere that had made them feel at home, belonging, a certain part of creation. Those who wanted to then related their experience to the group:

> *'Sitting alone and watching the tide go out into the sunset';*
> *'Running in the rain, dancing with it, on my own';*
> *'Being quiet and silent looking over the gate of my granny's garden';*
> *'The stillness of being awake in a safe warm bed, moonlight streaming through the window onto my feet.'*

Everyone's memories had one thing in common –
stillness . . . silence . . . aloneness . . .

Notes

[1]St John's Gospel, 3:7–8 (Jerusalem Bible). Quoting Jesus Christ's answer to the enquiries by Nicodemus about the birth of the spirit in each individual.

Part One: THE ACTIVITY OF STILLNESS

Chapter 1
THE STARTING POINT

'The trouble is . . .
. . . it's the noise.'
(Stay with it. What sort of noise?)
'Not just the lorries and the construction works and the piped music and the machines . . .'
(What sort of noise?)
'It's the arguments and the demands; having too much to do and trying too hard to get through it; it's having the news of other people's disasters and catastrophies in my living room; it's all the warnings of dangers, all the information of things that might happen to me, or my family. Then there are always the goads to do more, buy more, achieve more, get more . . .'
(Any other noise? Any other disturbance?)
Pause.
'The confusion . . . deep inside . . . the tangled voices . . . there's an agitation there; I try to block it off by smothering it; covering it up with even more — different — distractions. More doing . . . more noise . . .'
What can I *do* about all this noise?'

The world blares out its busyness and its importance and it screams for our attention. It challenges us to meet all its hows and whens and whys and wheres, coming at us and bursting through the boundaries of our personal space; it gets into our homes, our places of work, our shops and schools and offices, into our ears and heads and hearts, until it seems to be crowding our very being. Demanding us to be *doing*.

And we are stuck in the middle of it.

Too much of this sort of noise often results in headaches and irritability, lack of concentration and sleeplessness; but it doesn't end there. When the noise goes on unrelieved, people start wondering whether it's all worth it, what it's all really about. It's as if they had lost their bearings among the racket. We can become so distracted, so pulled apart and pushed around from every direction, that we hardly know who we are. People say things like, 'I feel lost, disconnected' or, 'I don't know where I am going any more'. So we lose sight of our sense of direction, of our sense of humour, and a sort of bewilderment gets into the very centre of who we feel we are.

This is the starting point. When the noise and disturbance is acknowledged and we can recognize the effect it is having on us, then the time has come to actually do something about it. Something can be done which makes the noise not only bearable, but makes out of it something that balances everything else in our lives.

This is a book of suggestions that are well-tried, realistic and practical. They will be concerned with the down-to-earth problem of clearing an area, a space where we can cultivate — what? Peace? Stillness? A sense of proportion? Somewhere where light gets in and laughter seems easier? Perhaps all of these. Many other books are full of theory, but this one is about the hows of growing a central core of assurance and strength which will support and feed our everyday living. It will be about how to live with too much doing, when the noise is part of the conditions in which we live.

There are several options at the start:

– We could just struggle on, doing the best we can. The difficulty about this is that while we do so we are probably becoming hardened and unaware that some long-term resentment is building up into a habit. Then there is a danger that we will grow into a 'Poor little me' sort of person.

- We could just blame everything else, claim that it is all outside of ourselves, and there is nothing that we personally can do about it; the difficulty about this is that while we are not taking positive steps to do something, our anger against the outside increases and builds up a sense of alienation towards the world in which we live. Then there is a danger that we will grow into an 'I don't like you, you're no good' sort of person.
- We could start a campaign against the most noticeable external noises, and work for the Noise Abatement Society, for instance; the difficulty about this is that while we concentrate on the external sources of noise, even to better them, we are probably not looking at the internal sources of noise. Then there is a danger that we will grow into an 'If only *they* would change' sort of person.
- We could do a bit of all these, but also decide to take some responsibility on ourselves for the effects of the noise. This may be simply a matter of clearing a space, of making a patch of time, where we can physically get away from the noise. Or it may be appropriate to think about getting to know the stillness that lies deeply within us; uncovering the well of stillness that we are born with but which gets smothered under the activities and strivings of growing up. It may be we'd like to tackle this exploration on our own, or we may prefer to do it sharing it with others. And having discovered this internal stillness, we may find we feel better equipped to deal with the external disturbance.

Whenever a group of people talk about the pressures they experience in their lives, the subject of how to reach into stillness very often comes up. Perhaps one person will mention it, rather gingerly, and straightaway others in the group will chime in. The subject is difficult to put into words, and it is commonly blanketed by a natural shyness; once it is mentioned and a corner of the blanket is lifted, the group will act with relief as though something very close to their hearts has been let out. Enquiries are made about a special sort of stillness. A place that is always near to hand, and yet is not obvious to outsiders. Somewhere to dip into for a quick bit of refreshment or refilling, but without needing to put on a special swimming costume or having to get to somewhere far away. To have a complete break from noise and bustle, and from people and responsibilities, is marvellous but it only happens occasionally. A total break away is like a feast, an event that is as rich and memorable as it is rare. The need expressed by everyday people is not for a distant sanctuary, or a hidden, out-of-this-world place; people are asking for a here-and-now, earthy, bread-and-butter and very practical sort of stillness, something that is immediate and accessible.

It is not just a matter of looking for a way through the busyness, nor simply of getting a rest from it. It's not just an occasional moment of respite that is needed, nor simply something that makes for a comforting cushion of quiet. What is being looked for is a stable, reliable, unshakeable central point, a core of stillness at the very centre of doing and of noise. If one is in a position of being able to withdraw, or to opt out, that is one thing; but the value of a refuelling unit that is there at the very centre of all that is going on, all the time, anywhere, any place, is without price.

Many people are expressing a hunger, a longing, a search for assurance, stability, stilling, centering. Those who find it have a way of instant refilling which helps them cope with all that comes at them in the noise.

The cartwheel is a good analogy:

As it goes along, the edge of the cartwheel has to contend with all that is lying in its path; it jolts noisily along the ruts through mud and puddles, meeting sharp stones and soggy sand, doing its best to get over any obstacles in the way. An ant clinging to the rim has a bad time of it; it gets splashed and battered, becoming confused and even dizzy with the speed.

Now, when the ant starts to crawl down one of the spokes which connect the edge of the wheel to the hub, it discovers that the speed of the circles it is going through becomes progressively slower. The mud and bumps and splashes are still there in the road, but the ant is less put out by them. The nearer it gets to the central hub, the less disturbed

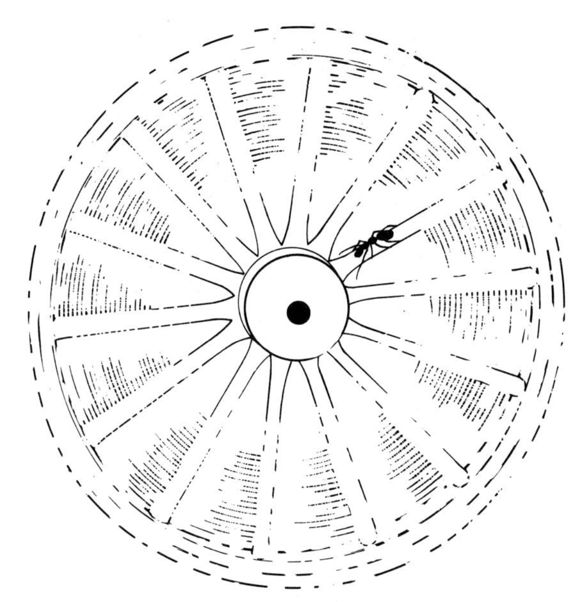

and the more collected it becomes. When the ant reaches the central point of the wheel, it is at a place where there is total stillness.

This now is the strongest point of the analogy: when the ant comes to the stillness at the middle of the hubbub, it discovers that this is the very point from which the wheel gets its direction and power. If the central point goes askew, the whole wheel topples over. If the input of power is not exactly centred, the whole cart goes awry. The absolute centre is not only totally still, it is of critical importance to the safe running of the whole wheel. In addition the ant finds that it is free to move up and down between the rim where all the action takes place, and the centre where the source of power and direction lies, whenever it likes.

There is a need to get in touch with our own withinness that belongs to everybody. Jung describes the drive we all have to 'attend to the reverberations deep within', but in our daily lives we easily become totally taken up with the tasks of making a living, keeping house, coping with pain, and finding entertainment. So we end up in what has been described by Laurens van der Post as 'a state of vast meaninglessness', and we busy ourselves simply to avoid looking into it. Even Scrooge, we are told in Dickens' *Christmas Carol*, kept himself too busy in order to protect himself from seeing things as they really were. When we have been wrapped up in busyness and noise we find it difficult to convince ourselves — and those living close to us! — that it is a priority to find time to cultivate a space to be still and to refuel. The fascinating thing is that as soon as this priority is fully experienced, it is at once easier to find time. And the more we manage to practise it, the easier the 'quick dip' becomes.

The following chapters will offer ideas on how to set about it. Whether the reader is someone who works in a large office with its competing demands and conflicting relationships, or a shop manager with objectives based on changing market trends, or a member of the 'caring professions' whose clients' needs seem unending, or a mother nurturing a growing family in sickness and in rude health, or a single person without a paid job — whatever the occupation or status or background of the reader, they should find something relevant in the following chapters, because they have grown out of the queries of just such people. And however each person reacts to things of the spirit, and whether they are attached to a named denomination or none, whether they are humanist or agnostic or atheist or a committed disciple, this book is about an experience that is common to them all. For we are all people living in the middle of our modern cult of Doing, and we all need to service that doing by Being.

But here's a note of warning: those who make a habit of dipping into stillness are liable to laugh more. Stilling doesn't have to be solemn; stilling makes for greater trust in living with uncertainty, it builds spontaneity and gaiety, it brings with it a freeing and a lightening; it becomes easier to play and to laugh — especially at myself and my pomposity. Colours are brighter, good cheer is righter, self-importance and solemnity no longer apply. It's something to do with loosening hope and trust and play into the world. It puts 'wisdom' and creativity side by side, where they belong. As Proverbs puts it:

> At the Creation, Wisdom was at the side of the Creator,
> His darling and delight,
> playing in his presence continually,
> playing over his whole world,
> when he made earth's foundations firm . . .
> whoever fails to find me deprives himself . . .
> happy are those who keep to my ways.
> (Proverbs 8:30, 36, 34)

Smiling and the still centre go together. Sometimes I just have to break out laughing . . .

Chapter 2

DOING AND STILLING – BALANCING THE 'HIGHS' AND THE 'DEEPS'

It's all a great balancing act. Unless I get to grips with this act, the pace and the speed I find outside myself is liable to overcome the space and the peace I want inside myself. So I have to take over the responsibility for it, if it is not going to overtake me.

Indeed, one of the greatest obstacles there is in getting to grips with this balancing act is to persist in believing that the disturbance I experience is *all* on the outside: if it is on the outside then it can remain someone else's responsibility. Someone else causes it, someone else can be blamed for it, somebody else should do something about it. It is only when I come to accept that the commotion – whatever its cause and wherever it comes from – does in fact reach into my own withinness, that I can start dealing with it myself. Once I know it is getting inside me, I can own it. I can realize how much it confronts me and confuses all my perceptions. So then I become not only the best person to deal with it, but I am also the person to gain the greatest benefit from having dealt with it. To become wholly in balance I can take charge of both sides, the doing and the stilling, with a foot on each side of the seesaw. And I will be in a position to laugh at myself when sometimes I topple over.

On the whole, we spend most of our lives in one of two states, both of them useful but each of them contrasting with the other. These states are closely allied to the functions of the two sides of the brain. The *left-hand hemisphere* of the brain is primarily concerned with functions that are highly prized in our Western society. We are trained to rationalize, judge, analyse, criticize, systematize, and those who are good at these things can command high salaries. We use the left-hand brain when we are aroused, when we are straining and striving, and whenever our thinking and behaviour is based on logic. We have grown up with social expectations that make this side of our personalities dominant, so these attributes are praised and raised to exertions almost beyond belief. Doing helps us to strive and arrive; to convince and to win; to justify and to prove. It tells us we can overcome and cover up and come again for more. In today's climate, it is those who are good at these things who win respect, get promoted, earn more money, receive higher status. Our society applauds them.

This side of our personality also takes on the exhausting task of having to respond, each second, to new situations, new questions, new issues; it is constantly buoying up our public self, proving and improving the image, getting Self noticed and appreciated.

But there is another, gentler, side to living. The *right-hand hemisphere* of the brain is concerned with functions that do not depend on reason and logic for their value: these are more about our 'gut' feelings and our intuitive understanding. Things like empathy; creativity; those deep meanings that are just 'known' rather than being provable; and a belief in a self that is valuable for its uniqueness quite apart from its cleverness. Our sense of mystery, of play, of laughter, of spontaneity stems largely from this part of the brain, and in cultures where meditation and collective wisdom are highly valued it is these areas that are commonly prized.

It would seem sensible to keep the functions of the left and the right brain properly balanced, but priorities in society today don't make this balancing act easy: in general it is those who work with things calling for creativity, caring, worship, and listening who get less pay than most. Those who work with numbers and measuring devices and well-defined

(to p. 8)

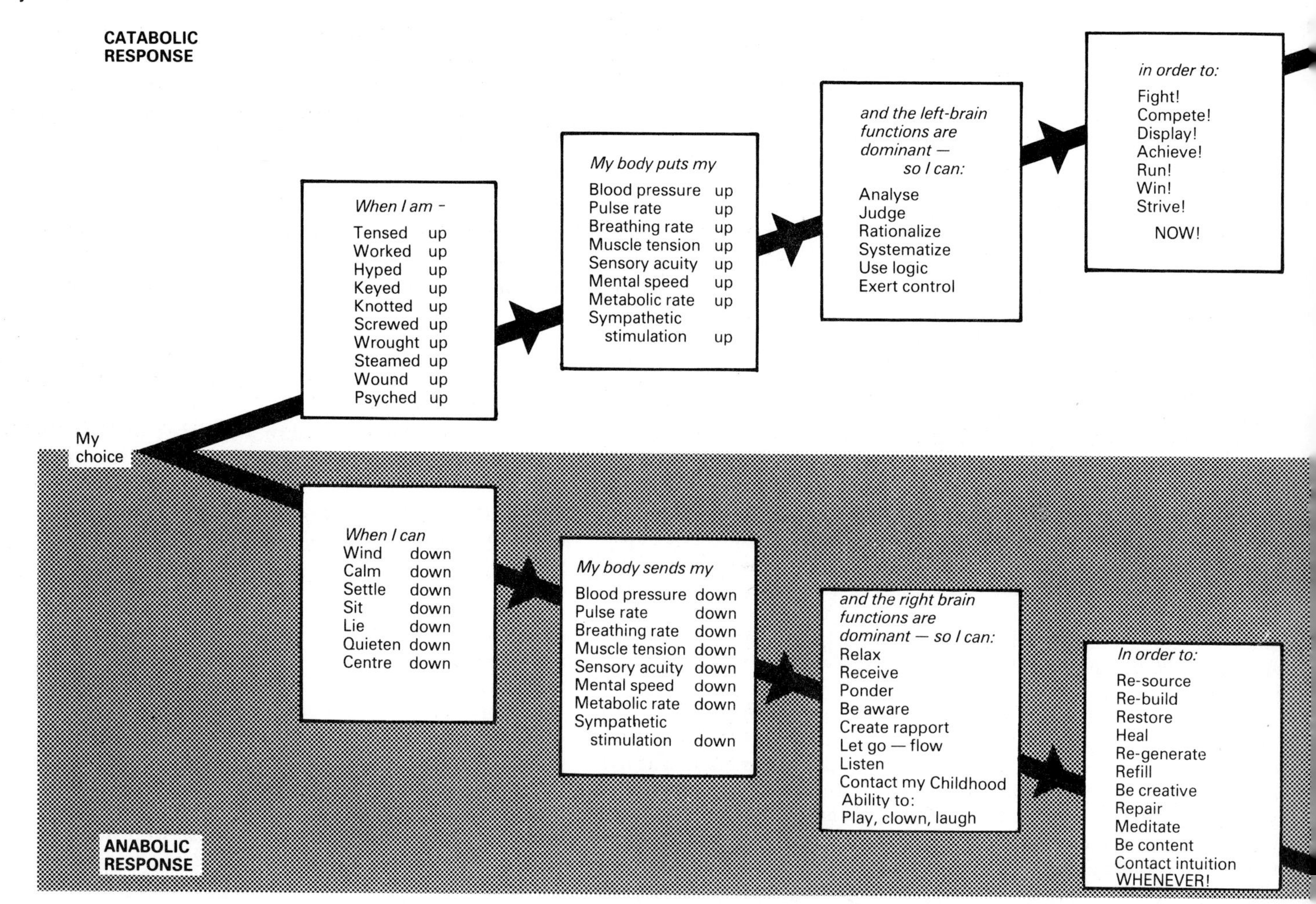
CATABOLIC
RESPONSE
When I am –
Tensed up
Worked up
Hyped up
Keyed up
Knotted up
Screwed up
Wrought up
Steamed up
Wound up
Psyched up
My body puts my
Blood pressure up
Pulse rate up
Breathing rate up
Muscle tension up
Sensory acuity up
Mental speed up
Metabolic rate up
Sympathetic stimulation up
and the left-brain functions are dominant — so I can:
Analyse
Judge
Rationalize
Systematize
Use logic
Exert control
in order to:
Fight!
Compete!
Display!
Achieve!
Run!
Win!
Strive!
NOW!
My choice
When I can
Wind down
Calm down
Settle down
Sit down
Lie down
Quieten down
Centre down
My body sends my
Blood pressure down
Pulse rate down
Breathing rate down
Muscle tension down
Sensory acuity down
Mental speed down
Metabolic rate down
Sympathetic stimulation down
and the right brain functions are dominant — so I can:
Relax
Receive
Ponder
Be aware
Create rapport
Let go — flow
Listen
Contact my Childhood
Ability to:
Play, clown, laugh
In order to:
Re-source
Re-build
Restore
Heal
Re-generate
Refill
Be creative
Repair
Meditate
Be content
Contact intuition
WHENEVER!
ANABOLIC
RESPONSE

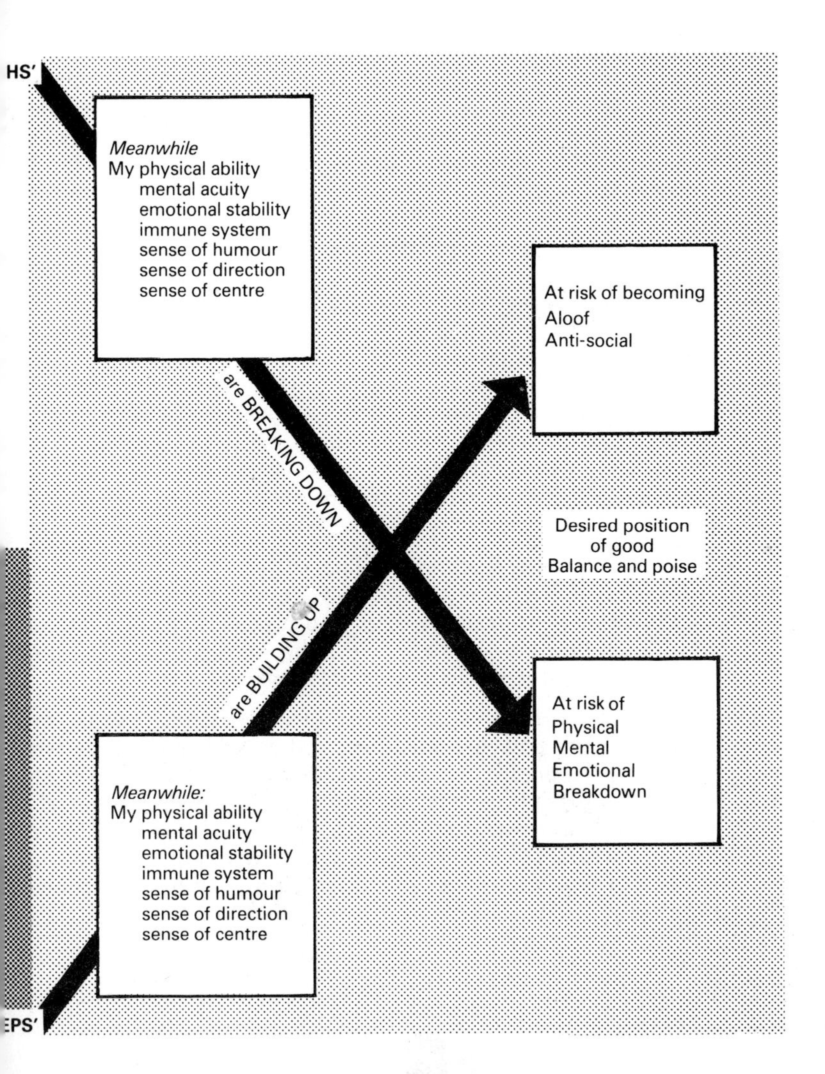

On the *physical* level, when we allow our muscular tension to wind down and let relaxation take over, all the systems of the body can be refreshed; all the channels which carry air, food, water, lymph, blood, and nerves can flow unobstructed; and healing and new growth can take place.

On the *emotional* level, when we allow our churned up feelings to calm down, their different strands get sorted out; we can take a step back from the apparent tangle, and then new and unexpected ways through it become clearer.

On the *mental* level, when we put on one side our judgemental skills and allow our speeding mental capacities to rest, or to focus on a single point, then we can bring fresh insights to the picture later. These may connect with important intuitive and creative functions that have been overlooked.

On the *spiritual* level, perhaps the most important of all, when we give up our dependence on words and deliberately quieten our verbal prayers, and if instead we tap into that deep part of us which is below the level of easy expression, then it becomes more possible for the Word itself to flow in through us.

precepts are those who receive more pay than most. So we don't get much encouragement to develop the functions of the right-hand brain.

There is a fascinating paradox about the way we ordinarily behave. Broadly speaking, at any moment we are either in an aroused state or in a contented state.

The *aroused state* (also known as the state of catabolic response) is when we take part in activities that stimulate and excite us; we may find this very enjoyable or we may find that we become overstretched and tense. Either way the amount of energy we generate goes up, and we call it getting 'high'. But, and this is astonishing, while we are engaging in this type of 'up' activity, our body tissues are in fact being broken down. While we might feel up, biologically speaking our physical resources are wearing down, our stores of emotional and mental energy are draining down, and our immune efficiency is being put down. If this type of activity continues without remission, we are at risk of breakdown. (The Greek prefix *cata* which is applied to the state of being 'high', means DOWN in position, quantity or degree.)

In contrast, the *contented state* (also known as the state of anabolic response) is when we allow ourselves to settle down – slowing down, sitting down, calming down; it is then that we can relax, reflect, restore. The amount of energy we generate goes down, but at the same time biologically speaking our body tissues are being built up and repaired, our emotional and mental resources are refilled, our immune efficiency is raised up, and energy is stored up. (The Greek prefix *ana* which is applied to the 'down' state, means UP, back again, anew.)

This astounding process can be put into diagrammatic form. As long as I am being stimulated – that is, working at getting to where I'm not yet then I am in the state called catabolic. This is fine when I want to be motivated, but the strain of it must be relieved at some time if breakdown is to be avoided. On the other hand, when I am musing, resting — that is, being contented for the moment with where I've got so far — I am in the state known as anabolic. This is when physiologically my bodily tissues are rebuilt, and the healing of knots and scars in my body, my emotions, and my spirit all speed up. It is at this level too, that I tap into my squashed-down child-like responses — things like trust and wonder, laughter and gaiety, hope and spontaneity, come welling back up again. I can even let go of my need to be in control. A friend exclaimed, 'How quickly one learns that having touched it for a moment, just one fragment of a moment, one can never do without it again!' It's great.

The whole process can be demonstrated on many levels, as the chart on pp. 6–7 shows.

The really notable thing about this chart is how it illustrates the way in which the activities of striving and busyness are contrasted with the practice of stilling. By counterbalancing the 'highs' with the 'deeps' we become better at coping on every level — physical, emotional, mental and spiritual — and also our lives become vastly enriched. But because the skills of stilling are now so smothered, we have to choose to learn and develop them in a deliberate way.

There are some questions which concern people about this sort of exercise:

- Is it 'selfish' to try to reach into stillness?
- If it helps me to live more comfortably, does it just benefit me?
- Is the practice of stillness only for those who have the time to spare, those who are self-engrossed, who are really looking for withdrawal from the world and its problems?

Living more 'comfortably' at the centre of doing actually means to be strengthened (with *com* strength *fort*), and perhaps those who are strengthened are of more use to others in their needs and troubles than those who are perpetually on the go. It's like being used as a funnel, an ordinary domestic plastic funnel, nothing fancy. A funnel doesn't have a lid, so it accepts everything, it rejects nothing, and then it concentrates whatever it has received into a stream with new direction. There is a special meditation on this in Part Two.

It is becoming a matter of the greatest urgency that we draw upon, draw in, as much of the goodness of creation as it is within our capacity to do; this urgency is partly for our own centering and affirmation, partly for the filling up of others, but largely for the lessening and weakening of the negative forces that powerfully surround us. Perhaps the more we are opened up so that the beneficient, creative power of God can flow through us, the more affronted will be the malevolent powers of which St Paul speaks. Today it is easy to conclude — as many do — that evil and disaster seem to have an upper hand in our everyday world; so it is crucial that we assent to the flowing of God's creative and regenerative power. Perhaps most of all, we need consciously to affirm it in the unseen, motivating, levels of experience which we all share.

That HE IS; and that he is A POWER
A PRESENCE
A PURPOSE,[1]
and that it is his way, his word, his will, that is paramount.

There is current a story which sums up the whole of this chapter: Some native porters were made by their masters to hurry through the African jungle (the Europeans had to get there, and anyway they were afraid of the hidden unknowns of the undergrowth). Suddenly the porters put down their loads and refused to take another step. When challenged and goaded they said, 'We will go no further at present. We have come so far and so fast that now we must wait for our souls to catch up with us.'[2]

NOTES

[1]Quote from the Rt. Revd David Jenkins, Radio 4, Christmas 1987.
[2]Related by Kate Compston in *Julian Meetings Newsletter*, Summer 1990.

Chapter 3

WHAT IN THE STILLNESS? THE PLACE OF NO WORDS

It is easy and natural to watch silently as waves ebb and flow on a beach, or to lean over a gate to see the sun go down. Just stopping talking opens up a world that was familiar to us before we learned to speak. Giving place to a state of no words should be as simple and friendly as that.

Yet, as adults, we commonly find difficulty in doing without words. We have used — and misused — words for a long time. As soon as we became conscious of the use of words we started to overuse them. We learnt to use words to compete for attention, to call out in alarm when there was no need, to demand by repeating and nagging and insisting. Later on we can become dependent upon that sort of continual noise; some of the most lasting memories of school are to do with the frustration of being told to 'shut up'. In adulthood, sounds and noises become so constant that we feel uneasy and even outraged when they stop, and our feelings about silence can be negative. If the continuous noise of a machine suddenly stops we think of danger; when silence falls on a group we say it's 'eerie'. As very young children we may have been happy with silence, but as we grow older we tend to build up the idea that it is something to be avoided.

But when silence is willed and wanted, then it sings.

The approach to silence can be brimming with questions:

Is the place of no words empty or full?
a threat or a relief?
inhibiting or releasing?
dark or light?
what happens?

There is a simple problem here: words are extraordinarily inefficient at describing no words. Art and music and dance can get in touch with things that are inexpressible more effectively than words can. There are so few words that are actually good at relaying what stillness is like. What stillness is all about is just being there, staying there, emptying, stripping, basking; *not trying*; forgetting about having to produce something; giving up the business of judging how I am doing, what I am doing, whether I am getting better at it, how I will know I have arrived. Just letting go and letting be. It isn't a case of being able to say — I've got it! — or — I've arrived! It's more like recognizing a core inside that is familiar, because it has been there all along.

Nor is it a case of looking for sensations or revelations; insights may arrive but they are not the goal. The goal is to access, to contact, my own withinness, that space where I am nearest what it is I was created to be. And where I will be the closest I can get to the indefinable God who created me. I will be tapping in to, and holding on to, the stillness of God deep within me.

Dame Julian of Norwich said, in the fourteenth century, 'It is full great pleasance to God that a silly soul come to him nakedly and plainly and homely.'[1] And Maria Boulding writes, in this century, 'His springing creativity is in me at the core of my being; his truth, his desire to give himself, his surging life and his will that creating should go on. My chaotic inadequacy does not deter him.'[2]

That should be enough. But in the face of our modern passion for justification perhaps a visual figure will make it easier. The analogy of the decks of a ship can be a telling one: the ship represents the whole of my life and what I choose to do with it.

At the top level, on the surface, is the DOING deck. Several things are happening:

- As captain of my own ship, I am standing at the wheel and steering.
- This is the activities deck, and everybody is very busy playing games; they are co-operating, or competing, or comparing. Just watching each other as happens in everyday living.
- There are lots of people around, but — and this is important — I am the only one who can use the speaking tube which connects this deck with whatever is happening on the decks below.

Many people stay on this top deck most of their lives.
Some of those who are very active in their lives find it difficult to get in touch with stillness.

The next deck is where the THINKING goes on. This is where:

- timetables of tides based on past experience are kept;
- maps to be worked on for our present journey are laid out;
- charts of unknown seas yet to be explored are stored.

ASSESSING and PLANNING are important functions in people's lives. Some people spend a great deal of their time with them; others use mental activity less.
Thinking has a role in some types of meditation, but while our mental processes are busy, our whole being is not totally in stillness.

The third deck is the FEELINGS area, where things happen which arouse our strongest emotions. These are represented by symbols such as:

- A dining-room table: for feeding and being fed; for family sharing (who is included? who isn't there?); for the preparation, and offering of gifts; are they received or rejected?
- A bathroom: this is where I keep myself 'clean' in private; it is where I try to make myself socially acceptable; it is where I get rid of those bits of me I don't like, and the bits that are 'waste'.
- A bedroom: this is where I relax, sleep, and make love, and it represents the very strong feelings I have about whether or not I do these things, and whether or not they are fulfilling.

Some people spend a lot of their lives just doing and feeling. They stay on those two decks.
A great deal of feeling can be experienced in silence, including feelings of devotion to God. But while our emotions are busy, we are not in total stillness.

Lower still is the ENGINE ROOM, and many people never get there at all. It is where whatever it is that gets me going gets on with it. It is where essential things exist, and essential things are happening, and it's important to get to know what they are. Such things as:

- The fuel and its storage; I have to be sure it's the right formula for me, that it's in the right amount, and that it is refilled.
- The different parts of the engine; I have to make sure that they are kept repaired and interacting smoothly with each other.
- The sound of the works; I have to stand still and listen, to make sure I understand it and that it complies with the designer's intentions.

This is the deck where the DRIVING FORCE of the ship connects to the propeller, which in turn affects the whole direction of the ship. This is where words are pointless at the hub of the noise.
This is where I may be encompassed and taken up by the existence of the whole. Some people may be given rich mystical experiences at this deeply submerged level; most people are content to just be and know.

Be still . . . and know . . . who is God.
Be still . . . and know . . . who God is.

There are a few extra points to note about this ship:

- The engine and its workings are below the waterline; they are seldom seen by onlookers.
- The engine is the only part of the inside of the ship that was designed by its maker, and was delivered with it — all the furnishings on the other decks were added later.
- The engine and its workings are connected to the propeller and the keel, which give the ship its direction and its stability. For me, Christ is the propeller and the keel.

When looking at our lives in this analogy, it is important to remember always that we are each and every one unique; that each individual has a different background, up-bringing, and unique set of genes; and that each individual has a different pattern of circumstances to live with. So there is no right/wrong about the level on which each of us is most comfortable; there is no ought/must about where we should spend most of our time (except, perhaps, a bit of exploration can help us to know ourselves a scrap better). The guiding slogan will always be — 'be as you can and not as you can't'.

God knows what he made, I don't have to show him, or explain it to him, or apologize that I'm not what he didn't make. In recognizing what level God made me for, there is no need to strive or prove or earnestly pretend; he knows where he wants me to be. There is a proper and critical distinction between acting as if I were a god, and behaving as if I were of God.

Some say that today it seems as though we put all our energies into working for a world of non-mystery. We push to find out as much as we can, but perhaps there comes a time for acknowledging that beyond all our understanding, and encompassing it, is a world of non-knowledge and wonder and amazement. A world of marvel. We could be a bit more pleased about unexplained mysteries, when we know that that is where we come up against the Other.

And sometimes, in the deep dark of the throat,
In the blackness, no-knowingness, of the pit of the stomach
Where no words, no images can qualify to be:
Where the qualities of me are put aside by that bit of God which is within me . . .
Where unwhole is with Whole,
then...
True weal wells.

NOTES

[1]Julian of Norwich, *Revelations of Divine Love* (trans. Dom Roger Hudleston). London, Burns Oates, 1927 (p. 9).
[2]Boulding, M., *The Coming of God*. London, Collins/SPCK, 1982 (p. 103).

Chapter 4

WHEN, HOW, AND WHERE?

So, we are looking for a special place, a layer within ourselves where we can find out what our real strengths are, where we can get in touch with our hunches that are too difficult to put into clear words. In fact it is:

– a place of light and lightness;
of warmth and assurance;
of holding and of being held;
of attentiveness and of being attended to;
a place of hope, and of good cheer.

This chapter will deal with purely practical matters. The hunger and thirst for silence and stillness can too easily get hung up on simple practicalities: things to do with timing and positioning, places and people. So now down to the brass tacks of making a space and a place for silence.

It all stems from how I set my priorities:
how much do I really want to make this space??

WHEN? MAKING TIME

Just *knowing* it can be done is all that matters, mixed in with a bit of determination and persistence. The following extracts from letters from ordinary people speak for themselves.

'When I'm busy physically, like washing up, cleaning, weeding, shopping, on the bus, I find I want to replace the continual chatter in my head with the single phrase, "Glory be to God".'

'In the War years it was fairly easy because my baby was tiny and I was getting up at 5-ish anyway to feed her and us, no one thought it was peculiar that I was dressed very early. And with the other four children being at school, I was able to leave her with them when they came home from school, and go and do a quick food shop and get in another half-hour's prayer at church on the way home, and still be back in time to get everyone's tea. I hope I wasn't being selfish – they adored the baby and really loved this time with her.'

'I said to myself, if I can find time to have a friend here for coffee now and again, I can find time to have people here to spend silence together. Which do I want most? A chat over coffee or stillness with tea?'

'For half an hour before breakfast every morning I seek to lay myself completely open to the Spirit, trying to abandon all natural thought. The danger of using words is that one stays just outside the inner sanctuary concentrating on that one attribute of God. This can become an obstacle in the way of knowing God himself . . . I think this way only suits some people. I just happen to be one of them.'

'Commuting in the train is the best time. It's regular, you know just how much time you've got, there are no demands being made on you, there are no interruptions, and others take it for granted you're having a nap!'

Other suggestions for making time for centering include:

- parking the car in a lay-by for a few minutes on the way home from work;
- using the silence of the early-morning feed needed by a young baby;
- while gardening;
- making use of any regular period of waiting, whatever its cause;
- whenever there is a patch of night wakefulness;
- simply getting up earlier, or doing without a cooked breakfast;
- being quiet, on one's own in the park, or in the restroom, during the lunch break at work;
- putting the alarm on for the early hours, getting out of bed to spend some time in the silence with God, then getting back into bed to finish off the night's sleep.

In the USA, some highly-paid business executives are given time at the office before they start work to be still. The companies involved find their employees become more productive this way, so the time is cost-effective.

It is perhaps a counsel of perfection to suggest that 20–30 minutes can be put aside every night and every morning to be still, but a very great number of ordinary people do do it. Some try to make a habit of getting to work a little earlier than their immediate colleagues, and finding quiet at their desks. And some people find that thinking in terms of a *weekly* amount of time spent in reaching for stillness — for instance a total of two hours broken into three or four blocks — fits more easily into their lives. The idea of working on a weekly total, instead of daily bits, can be especially helpful where time is also made for reading and liturgy. Finding the space when there are young children around will be looked at in Chapter 7. But, given the will, space can be made, it can be done. After all, if it is God's time, and if he wills you to have it, it will be there.

HOW? THE APPROACH AND POSITIONING

In theory, the still centre can be found anywhere. In practice, given all the blustering and battering that is going on around us, it makes sense to make it as easy as possible for ourselves. Some people find it quite simple: just by sitting quietly and well-supported in an upright chair and breathing regularly, they can quickly come into contact with their own withinness. Others find that to shed all one's immediate concerns is more difficult, and they want to go about it in a more ordered way. The following suggestions are for them. Not all these ideas have to be taken on board, but they are all well-tried and tested and found to be reliable.

Using a lead-in

Different approaches suit different temperaments and situations. These are some of the ways that are used:

- *music*; this should be gentle and regular, without sudden jolts and surprises in rhythm or theme. Baroque music or Gregorian chants are excellent, also quiet guitar playing or music that sounds like flowing water;
- there is a special sort of *chanting*, practised by Buddhist monks, and another type sung by the community at Taizé, which is particularly helpful as a lead-in to silence;
- gentle *reading* or *poetry*, but something without great novelty or new ideas that can be too exciting;
- soft, slow *movement* in dancing or in stretching exercises. Many people find the concentrated holding-stretch used in yoga body exercises helpful; they can be useful for releasing physical tension and focusing the mind;

- *relaxation* techniques of various designs; these may be based on:
  - the joints and their movements, or
  - the muscles and their tension and release, or
  - the imagination and its power to relax the body, or
  - the use of the breath.

  Tapes are a popular way of overcoming the difficulty of reading a technique while the eyes are closed.*
- *breathing awareness* can be used on many levels:
  - if the breathing comes from low down in the body and makes use of the diaphragm, it will bring into play all those hormones which slow down the 'excitable' responses of our systems, both physical and mental (see Chapter 2);
  - counting breaths acts in a way that stills other thoughts;
  - listening to one's own calm, regular inhaling and exhaling — being aware of taking in positive, refreshing air and letting go of negative, exhausted air — can greatly help to settle any feelings that have been upset;
  - when we are feeling anxious, or stressful, a long slow exhalation will restore the natural balance of oxygen and carbon dioxide in the blood stream.

  Breathing exercises can affect us through the body, the mind, and the emotions – it is always more important to attend to breathing out, than to breathing in. The body will invariably refill itself with the level of breath that it needs after the lungs have been emptied; it is a mistake to go on 'topping up' the air in the lungs by trying continuously to breathe in. All too easily we can get into this habit of over-breathing without realizing it. Being over-conscious of breathing can create difficulties for some, so if this becomes a distraction just leave it alone. As one expert put it: 'As long as you're breathing both in and out you're doing OK'!

*Readers can write to the author at C.O.R.S. c/o 50B Hyde St., Winchester, Hants., SO23 7DY for her tapes of relaxation techniques. Cost £3.60. Please specify preference for secular or Godward language, and include a strong self-addressed and stamped envelope for prompt despatch.

The positions

Equally, different postures are preferred by different people. These are some of them:

- *sitting* relaxed in a comfortable arm chair: head up and balanced on the top of the spine, knees uncrossed and at right angles to the body, feet flat on the floor. Hands are usually kept lying open and receptive on the lap, or with one hand resting in the open palm of the other, thumbs just touching — whichever position makes it easier to forget about them!
- *lying*: on the floor or on the bed, with or without cushions, in a position that makes for total support and relaxation; then the body and its aches are not a distraction. Many people prefer to lie flat on their backs, perhaps with a cushion under the knees to raise them slightly; others like to lie on their front, arms down the side, and faces turned sideways (to relieve any pressure on the nose!). If at the same time the mind is kept focused and alert, sleep will stay away.
- *'kneeling'* on a meditation stool. It astonishes many people how comfortable this is: there is no constriction anywhere, and because the bony pelvic circle is slightly tipped to the front, the whole spine takes up the long 'S' curve in which it is primarily designed to be, and all the muscles attached to it can take their full share in supporting the trunk. So no external cushioning is needed. All the internal organs — heart, lungs, stomach etc. — function more freely in this position because there is no pressure on them from the outside. All systems can flow unobstructed: body, mind, feelings and spirit. A good way to make sure the spine is in the correct position is to imagine a strong magnet in the ceiling above pulling up your whole trunk — stretching up from the lowest part of your back, up through each of the vertebrae, through the back of your neck, stretching up

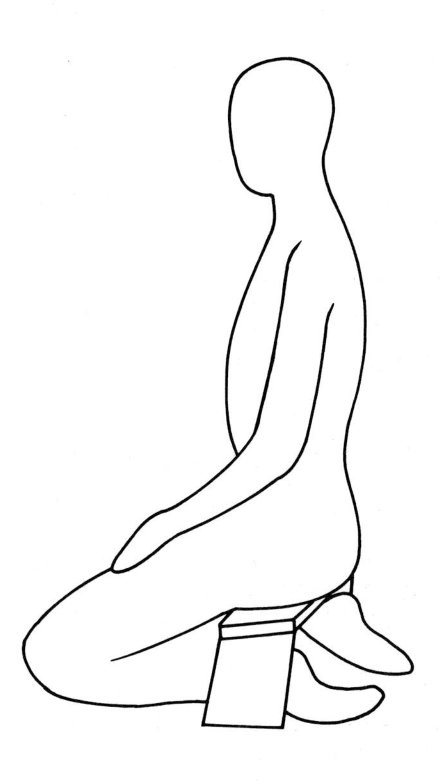

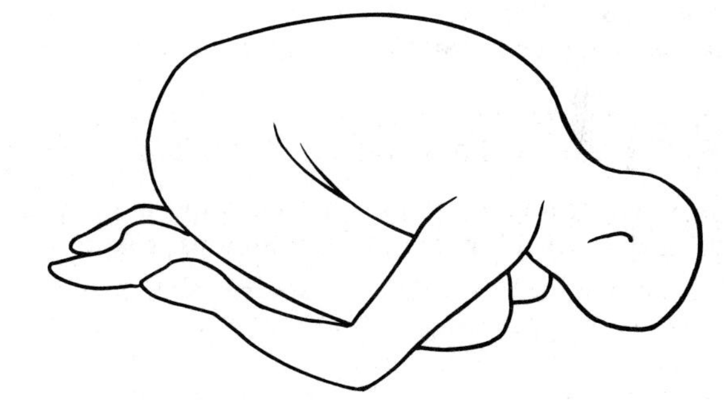

behind the ears (chin in, not up) — as if you were trying to touch the ceiling with the crown of your head. When the fullest stretch has been reached, then just let it all settle back into a comfortable position, keeping the upward direction. With practice, the whole body can stay there indefinitely, balanced without movement and without discomfort. The stillness and peace of mind brought about by using a meditation stool can affect one's entire life.*

- an excellent position that is less familiar is called that of the '*child*'. It has all the advantages of the above positions and an added bonus in that it is something special, set apart, for the particular activity of meditating.

And then, from a letter from a Classics graduate '. . . silence just comes, and I am able to let it come and stay, and just be, for a while, like a small child — or like a kitten, which gazes entranced at whatever catches his eye and stays silent and attentive.'

WHERE? PLACES

Some people can reach a state of inner stillness when they are walking or running or cycling on their own; still aware of what is going on around them but letting go of the analytical and judgemental side of their lives. While they allow the other, intuitional side to surface, they can just hold themselves empty of 'thought', in the secure presence of creation.

To a lot of people, however, it is very important that something definite marks a place which is set aside for stillness, something that makes it special for that purpose. It can be a simple candle on the floor; it might be a particular mat or stool or chair; it may be a special tree or place in a garden; it may be a picture or a crucifix. If this reminder is portable it can act as a signpost to stillness wherever it is taken. Alternatively, one particular spot such as a corner of a room or a church will carry extra associations of stillness and peace within it. Making a habit of being still in one place or with a certain object brings its own reminders.

Whenever, however, and wherever the practice of stillness becomes a habit, the person doing it will find they become more assured, more centered, and more convinced that in time 'all shall be well, and all shall be well, and all manner of thing shall be well'; so gradually good cheer will become the mainspring of their daily lives.

When considering how actually to fit stillness into the centre of doing, it helps to remember a story told of Jung. It is said that however full his diary became, whatever the demands made on him by others, and wherever he travelled in the world, he had one unalterable appointment. His secretaries were told he was never, on any account, to be disturbed during this daily appointment. It was an appointment he held with himself.

*Stools can be plain or polished, with supports that are fixed or folding, so they are portable and postable. Readers who may be interested in getting a stool like this are asked to contact the following address for details: Bernard Holley, 38 Sagecroft Rd., Thatcham, Nr. Newbury, Berks., RG13 4BD.

Chapter 5

WITH WHOM IN THE SILENCE?

More and more people are finding support in sharing silence together. Silence can be greatly strengthened if it is shared. Using silence for centering by oneself is like daily bread and butter; sharing silence in a group is like having a regular feast. How it happens comes from experience, and the only way to make sure it 'works' is to go ahead and try it. People are generally happier to close their eyes and be still in a setting of total trust, so fellowship and mutual confidence are essential. It is much less important that people should come from the same organization, or the same social background, or the same neighbourhood. It is much more important to share the same purpose: there is a Regency church in the City of London where business men in their pinstripe suits, and office staff in their pencil skirts, are content to lie on the floor in their lunch hour, totally relaxed, because they all share a common desire to become centered. There is an anecdote[1] about an alarmed cathedral caretaker who rushed into the Administrator's office because he had come across the Bishop and the Verger lying flat on their backs in the vestry — had they *both* had heart attacks? . . . ! They had simply been still together. Wherever people trust each other, and they agree to reach for stillness together, the depth of the silence that is shared is profound.

GROUPS — THE PEOPLE, THE TIMING, PLACE, AND STRUCTURE

'Open Centres' of all sorts are springing up all over the country.[2] These are people who want to create a sense of the depth and the mystery of life together, and their form is very varied. There are also over three hundred Julian Groups in Britain alone, with people meeting informally and ecumenically to spend time in silence with Christ. There are nearly as many John Main groups, made up of people who use a mantra as a means of coming close to the heart of God. The Quaker, or Friends', Meetings share a similar experience of silence. The numbers of denominational meditation groups and non-aligned shared silence groups and classes must run into thousands. The basic element of them all is that people *want* to sit together, still and relaxed, opening up and listening, in the place of no words.

That is, a place of welcome and being welcomed;
of trust and being trusted;
of being, instead of only doing.

Who with? The group of people

It is virtually impossible to draw up guidelines of *how* to find like-minded people with whom to share silence. Just looking out for people with similar ideas is not enough, since this is how people who are the most surprising supporters of silence get cut out. An open invitation can risk bringing in people who may rock the boat, but on the other hand those who don't gel with the group easily will just stop coming. Perhaps the best way is to ask people indirectly, such as — 'I know there are lots of different ways of getting together, but sometimes I feel I'd like to just be still, without too many words; I'm hoping to get some people to think about it, how would you feel?' Sometimes it is useful to start off by asking someone who has run groups to come and talk about it over a cup of tea, and invite friends in to join in the discussion. But each group will form its own ways of doing things and build up its own character, so the opinion of one person mustn't be imposed. Like Topsy, the group allegiance will just grow.

Before deciding whether to ask a certain person to a group, it may be appropriate to imagine the following situation — it is offered diffidently but can be a practical guide:

*Picture to yourself a car almost colliding with another car: the immediate response that is likely to be made in a near-miss situation like this will probably be something like — 'Thank God, it's alright, nothing really damaging happened', or, alternatively 'You ***, it's all your fault, can't you look where you're *** going?'*

Those who react in the first way are more likely to want to share stillness and to add to a group than those who tend to react in the second manner.[3] The person who more often gives thanks internally, is more likely to enjoy inwardness than the one who throws out blame externally. Perhaps surprisingly, it has very little to do with whether a person is articulate or garrulous or shy or retiring — any of these can be absorbed into a group and add to its fulfilment.

Numbers/Place

A 'group' can be anything from three to 30 people. They may all meet on a regular basis, but more commonly something between four and 15 will actually meet together at any one time.

The group can meet in someone's house: neither children nor animals are a deterrent to deep silence. Babies, infants, dogs and cats all enjoy profound stillness as long as they know that this is what is expected of them, and that everyone present is going to be still too. Given the chance and a confident lead, they will all settle down to stillness — an exception being goldfish, which in the author's experience resolutely continue to move!

Sometimes part of a hall can be screened off to give it an atmosphere of containment, or a chapel may be used where people can be in a circle rather than separated in rows. Most often, groups meet in people's homes.

Timing

Groups I have known have met:

- early on a weekend morning, at 7.30 a.m. before the family activities really get going;
- mid-morning on a weekday, while the children are at school;
- during the lunch hour, each member bringing their own simple packed lunch, so that those who go out to work and those who work at home can share stillness together;
- early afternoon before collecting the children from school;
- late afternoon, while the television is absorbing the family and before the evening meal has to be prepared;
- during the evening, at the ordinary time of evening meetings;
- for a specified time before or after other planned meetings;
- at 9 or 9.30 p.m., when the chores of the day are completed, other members of the household are settled or resting, and in the place of night prayers. This is a particularly beneficial and restorative time, and it can lead to a long peacefulness that lasts throughout the night.

Format

It is very important that the format of the meeting is agreed and understood by all who attend. The details of how the available time is going to be spent should be made clear to every newcomer or visitor.

For instance:

- Many groups choose to begin with a short time of conversation, exchanging news and general concerns; others prefer simply to step into quiet from the start, as if going to any service in church.

- Often a group will start or end with some sort of shared refreshment, but this is by no means necessary.
- Some groups like to have a theme for discussion, something offered by a member or a pre-arranged part of a book or reading; others prefer to allow a spontaneous idea to come up at the time. Either way, this theme will lead into the silence, perhaps using a familiar centering phrase or sentence; some suggestions for these are to be found in Part Two.

The actual time spent in silence will differ between groups. It may be agreed that:

- every 5 minutes the theme should be re-stated, or built upon; or
- 10–25 minutes will be spent totally uninterrupted; or
- some groups would prefer to stay at a level of silence where interruptions are acceptable and not startling; these vocal additions are sometimes known as 'words of the spirit'. This sort of silence is practised by the Society of Friends.

Diversions

Some common and familiar physical difficulties are bound to come up from time to time.

- If an itch becomes unbearable, what then? To scratch or not to scratch?
- If a rumbling tummy feels to its owner to be distracting others, should it be removed from the room? To stay or to go?
- If repeated swallowing becomes necessary and sounds like thunder to the swallower, what to do? To cough or to choke?
- If the telephone rings, should it be answered or left to haunt the group?
- If the birds outside, the children playing in the garden, the drill in the street, the neighbours' radio, interrupt the interior stillness, should it be stopped? How do you stop the birds singing?

Strangely, the answer to all of the above diversions is the same – *relax*. The itch will go of its own accord if it isn't given attention; the rumbles will cease as the whole body quietens and deep relaxation reaches its centre; the urge to swallow will stop as relaxation and calm touch the throat muscles (sometimes it is a useful tip to drop the chin down a little lower when this is a problem – gravity will draw the aggravating moisture away from tickling the back of the throat); outside noises will simply float onto the edge of consciousness and be totally undisturbing as concentration deepens. It is rather like selecting specific stimuli, the ones not selected just fade away. It is also useful to use a bit of common sense; of course scratch or cough or leave the room when necessary, and unplug the telephone or put it on the answering machine for the time of silence.

The trick is neither to deny nor repel distractions. Just allow them to become unimportant, not worth any sort of agitation, and they will pass of their own accord. Fighting them only gives them priority: don't fight, and they will wither away.

One of the greatest things about sharing silence is that each person is free to use it in the way that suits them best, but all are in the stillness together. Some may simply rest in the quietness, while others may have mystical experiences, but *nobody* is going to be 'offended' at the way another uses words. No one is going to be able to say – Oh! I wouldn't have put it like that – so in the silence those with different temperaments and different backgrounds really can draw closer together. And then there is no more to do than, in Dame Julian's words, sit still 'and enjoy in his love'.

Some groups choose to end their meetings with a joint slow repetition of the Lord's Prayer and the Grace, and a quiet immediate leave-taking; while others like to 'share' around the circle before they depart.[4]

There is no right or wrong way of using the time: the only really important thing is that the whole group should experience the stillness that they have come to seek, and not leave feeling that they have 'missed out'. The fundamental agreement – and perhaps the only fundamental agreement necessary, more so than holding a common spiritual belief and certainly more important than a common denominational allegiance – is that (from another letter) 'the group meeting is a public acknowledgement that this "thing" is important – the value of the centre where God and Self meet'.

So, having looked briefly at the practicalities of reaching for stillness within the commotion, we can move on to what different spaces there are within that stillness.

NOTES

[1]Harding, Geoffrey, *Lying Down in Church*. London, Churchman Publishing, 1990.

[2]Addresses for information about groups who use silence include: OPEN CENTRES, Avils Farm, Lower Stanton, Chippenham, Wilts., SN14 6DA.
JULIAN MEETINGS, 32 Grosvenor Rd, Norwich, NR2 2PZ.
CHRISTIAN MEDITATION CENTRE, 29 Campden Hill Rd., London, W8 7DX.

[3]This says something about internal and external locus of control.

[4]There is a problem attached to 'sharing' comment after sharing silence: what happens in the silence is very individual and very private to that individual, so there can be a tendency to spend some of the silent time working out what it is that is proper to be said in 'public' afterwards. Besides, a lot of what happens in the silence is not measurable, or judgeable, or even expressible in words, and it is a pity to spend the time 'watching' oneself and what might be 'happening'. Nonetheless, if there is a strong *joint* agreement in a particular group that post-silence sharing is useful, there is nothing more against it. If there are discussion and/or refreshments before going into silence it will be a group responsibility to make sure no one person dominates.

Chapter 6
WHICH SORT OF SILENCE?

'Call him or call him not — God is present.'
(Ascription carved around the front door of Jung's house.)

It comes as quite a surprise to find that there are as many spaces in silence — that is, the area below the level of words — as there are different types of personality or different sorts of development; each of these spaces has a particular way of being reached, and each way has its own enthusiasts who will insist that it is the 'best'. As *methods* of getting into stillness they each have their merits. However, effectiveness isn't all that counts, and whether *meaning* is attached to the method or not, and what that meaning represents, is an important issue. That question will be explored after a brief run down of the methods which are popularly used for tapping into stillness.

Sometimes there is confusion between the personal time out that is spent on self-questioning and analysis, and that which is spent in stillness. The former is a mental and emotional activity, one of self-searching; the latter is a discipline which is an activity of accepting, centering, and grounding. It is perhaps the difference between 'Am I loved? Could I make myself more lovable?' and *knowing* I am accepted, loved, lovable, loving — in spite of all my faults and inadequacies. Stilling is not examining and questioning, which is useful in developing my head-knowing and my heart-knowing; through stilling I tap into my *gut-knowing*. It is there that I can accept that we are *all* imperfect, but that equally the great God of creation loves us all, unconditionally. It is as I become rooted in this conviction, this assurance, that I can serve him and my neighbour better. All is gift; it is not dependent upon my own efforts to deserve God's love. People have devised various ways of switching into this stillness, because they have found it is not a switching-off from difficulties but a switching-in to deep, deep assurance.

METHODS

It would be over-simple to make out that there are strong divisions between the following methods: most of them overflow into each other. Even the terms used are sometimes interchangeable, and users of the titles 'meditation' and 'contemplation' often disagree about which word applies to which practice. Words are notoriously inept at describing the place of no words. Nonetheless, a few signposts into that vast area of discovery may be useful, and may help to make the different spaces in silence more recognizable.

All methods of becoming still start from a state of relaxation. Sometimes just being quiet and easy and undisturbed is enough; as experience grows, so a deeper degree of physical relaxation may be reached. Relaxation implies that the muscles of the body are not just resting easily, but that they are in a state of deep relaxation, deep restoration and deep healing. Meanwhile the mind is alert and wide-awake — there is no sense of sleepiness in real stillness.

Mulling

Resting passively inside oneself; day-dreaming, focusing on something good and pleasant. Being content with things as they are for this moment, contained in the here and now. Everybody with any sense of awareness does this from time to time.

The 'point' of just mulling is brought out in one of Tony de Mello's stories:

> Everyone became alarmed when they saw Mullah Nasruddin, astride his ass, charging through the streets of the village.
>
> 'Where are you off to, Mullah?' they asked.
>
> 'I'm searching for my ass', said the Mullah as he whizzed by.[1]

Heightened sensory awareness

This is a technique that can easily be learned and it has two main aims: to raise the sensitivity of one's senses towards the things that are around, and to provide detachment from things that are being stressful. That is, to switch on to the sensory messages that ordinarily we cut out when we have to be busy, and at the same time to switch off all the over-strain that goes with being too busy.

The method involves sitting still and comfortable, and 'opening up' the eyes, or ears, or sense of touch, or sense of smell, to all the myriad stimuli that are around and that we usually 'select out' because we cannot manage to attend to them all at once. Sometimes holding a shape in the hand is a help, and really getting to know its feel, texture, warmth, and comfort, and imagining what it might be like to be *that shape. Spending 10 minutes doing nothing but getting to know that shape, or those sounds through the window, or that small patch of carpet. Being still in this way brings great release and enrichment. Making a habit of it means that this type of calm appreciation of the here and now can be triggered simply by holding the familiar shape, or recalling the familiar 'switch', whenever it is wanted.*

Words like 'mindfulness' and 'heedfulness' have been attached to this sort of practice. Overheard at a business conference: 'It gets me on my way with a smooth mind.'

Self-exploration

Introversion: taking time out quietly to examine my own motives and actions and the emotions that fuel them is a valuable task. Most of us are easily fascinated by our own workings, and this type of exploring can have positive results: it can let in new light to help make better choices in the future, and it can bring a greater understanding when others react in a puzzling way. If the fascination of myself becomes a narcissistic obsession, then it no longer strengthens the stillness inside; the behaviour which results from self-exploration is then more likely to be negative, because it becomes self-absorption, it is self-seeking and spirals inwards; self-knowledge on the other hand spirals outwards, bringing greater comprehension of, and compassion for, other people.[2]

There is a fundamental difference between being egotistical, and ego-offered. Two people knew they were each untidy. The one allowed visitors to see into her only tidy room; the other welcomed friends anywhere. The first one didn't get to know anyone, she remained proud and isolated; the other was known through all the neighbourhood, and her friends were numberless. 'I'm lonely' said the one; 'I'm not much good at keeping tidy' said the other.

Discursive meditation

This is a type of mental exercise that has been used by Christians for centuries to deepen their understanding of life. There is a growing appreciation of the practice, using a method which exercises imagination as much as reason. It is a technique that follows certain stages:

A story, parable, or picture is chosen, which usually comes from some Scriptural or classic writing; it is read quietly and with great concentration, and then put on one side. Each part of the incident is looked at mentally, using any facts and knowledge that are at hand. Then the meditator imagines him/herself to be one of the characters in the story, and empathizes with the responses of some of the other people in it too. Lastly, some piece of this understanding is applied in imagination to real life; to stay with it, observe and feel what might happen. No hurry, no rush; but after a little while there may emerge something like a new conclusion or resolution that can be carried into everyday life.

As a means of achieving stillness at the centre of doing, this technique is useful when the incident chosen is one which leads to reassurance and peace.

Visualization

There is considerable coverage of this technique in the ordinary media at present. It is used in various complementary therapies to 'fight' serious illness, or confront phobias, or raise confidence, or simply provide a respite from stress. In terms of reaching a place of quiet within, the technique is straightforward.

Sitting or lying very relaxed and with the knowledge that there will be no interruption, the visualizer brings to mind a scene — either from real life or from the imagination — which represents peace and confidence and contentment. All thoughts and images that are outside this scene are gently told to wait in the wings, and one becomes immersed in the single, static, scene only. One can use a repeated mental formula, such as 'I am at peace, content and calm', which reinforces concentration on the theme. Every sensation and experience is focused on the one scene.

As a means of stilling many people find this practice extremely useful.

Insight meditation

In very general terms this is a method in which the deepest level of the intuition is allowed to surface, and hints and hunches about how to solve a problem emerge that are generally unexpected. It is a process that can be tried by believers or non-believers alike; believers are more likely to give thanks to an 'external' or supernatural wisdom as the source of their inspiration, while so-called non-believers will attribute the ideas to their 'inner resources'.

At its simplest this method involves emptying oneself of all preconceived ideas and sensations; simply waiting, listening, expectant, until symbols or associations float up from the unconscious layer of the personality — or indeed from folk consciousness. These images may bring clues to new ways of looking at things simply by connecting relationships that wouldn't have been thought up by reason alone. Dreams and memories can also play a large part in insight meditation.

Those who practise this technique regularly tend to develop a strong sense of their own being, and they become confident in taking a measured pace to life and have less tendency to 'flap'. As a friend put it to me: 'It's not a way out. . . . it's a way in.'

Self-hypnosis

This is a learnt strategy whereby confidence and calm are strengthened, and common feelings of being able to cope or being weak and unwanted are countered.

As before, relaxation is a necessary starter. A trained hypnotherapist can induce deep relaxation by using countdowns or alternating eye movements, but once this has been demonstrated to be effective the person can do it for themselves. Then a single phrase — 'I am competent/confident/capable/calm' is repeated for a specified time before the countdown is reversed and the session completed.

For some people this technique brings great release from their own fixed ideas of low self-worth or incompetence. Those who practise it can recall their improved attitude on demand: whenever they want to they can bring into their minds a shorthand trigger which takes effect instead of going through the whole routine.

Symbol meditation

Very many people use symbol meditation as a regular part of their lives, quite unselfconsciously. Anything that brings with it a meaning which is beyond itself is a symbol, and as soon as we look at these 'beyond' associations, we are meditating. Looking into the fire, receiving a red rose, watching a stream, thinking about a child's first shoe, standing in front of a cross, all give rise to symbol meditations.

It is a simple matter of focusing on the symbol, and drawing out of it ideas that are related and significant. The symbol then becomes the carrier of a package of ideas which the brain no longer has to keep in mind separately. This can be both a rich form of meditation, and a powerful means of centering.

There are some examples of symbol meditations in Part Two.

Using a mantra or mandala

The practice of emptying the mind and the emotions of everything other than a short phrase, one word, one image, or one pattern, has been practised down the centuries.[3] Since the comparatively recent introduction of transcendental meditation to the West, the terms 'mantra' and 'mandala' have become more familiar. Once again it is a technique of focusing attention, of allowing all other thoughts, distractions, concerns, to stand aside while the single mantra takes centre-stage.

The method can come immediately and naturally to some, while others have to struggle with conflicting images and ideas and demands for a considerable time. For some people the discipline isn't worth it, while others come to feel that the daily time spent with their own mantra is the mainstay of their living. Some experts insist that the mantra should be a sound totally without meaning, while others point out that if the mantra comes to stand for peace or emptying it has itself acquired meaning; so giving it a meaning in the first place is no bad thing.

As a focus a mantra can be used that has several meanings; examples of this kind of multi-layered word are given in Part Two.

Contemplation

This is an emotive word which sparks off different reactions in different users. It is a description of the end state which is just being, basking, waiting; becoming engulfed, engrossed, enclothed by that which is being contemplated – most powerfully of all by God, the creator of all.

Some people reach this goal by thinking about God, some people just manage to be with God with no thoughts. There is a difference between *knowing about* something and *knowing* it. Hence the famous remark of Carl Jung: 'I don't believe in God, I know him.'

To quote from Tony de Mello again:

> A salt doll journeyed for thousands of miles overland, until finally it came to the sea.
> It was fascinated by this strange moving mass, quite unlike anything it had ever seen before.
> 'Who are you?' said the doll to the sea.
> The sea smilingly replied, 'Come in and see'.
> So the doll waded in. The further it walked into the sea the more it dissolved, until there was only very little of it left.
> Before that last bit dissolved, the salt doll exclaimed in wonder, 'Now I know who I am!'[4]

For Christians, any of the above methods can be the route for them to reach this goal; to those without such a named allegiance, any of the above methods can be used to achieve stillness at the centre of doing.

Just a word on **DISTRACTIONS**. When someone is preoccupied with very many concerns, or is anxious about a particular problem, or is used to thinking about a lot of things at once, it can be difficult to concentrate for long on one picture or word or theme. This is a common experience; but what is equally common is that the less it is seen as a problem, the less it will become one. When I look at an aquarium for instance, there is one particular fish that grabs the whole of my attention. I watch him and follow him whatever he does, although I am well aware that there are other fascinating creatures living in the same tank, and they flit across my sight from time to time. I also know that I can pay attention to them later on. So for now, for this particular moment, I let the others flow past unlooked at, and keep all my interest focused on my one chosen fish.

COMING OUT

It is extraordinarily important, whatever method of stilling is used, to have a formalized way of returning to the hustle and demand of normal life. There can be a sense of sudden shock if it comes back too abruptly, and this can cause physical discomfort, dizziness, and confusion; worst of all, all that has been gained may be lost. Coming out should be done gently and gradually; some people have a kitchen timer with a muted 'ping' to warn them that the time is up; some people have a cassette tape on which they have recorded timed silence, at the end of which quiet music is faded in; with practice, most people develop a 'natural' sense of when the desired time is up; whatever means is chosen, an alarm clock should be avoided!

Generally, the agreed time for silence takes on a rhythm of its own and one can sense the passing of time without checking with a clock. However, having a set length is necessary to avoid either self-indulgence or exhaustion, and more positively to enable one's inner working to pace itself.

Within a group, one person is usually allocated the responsibility of keeping half an eye on the time, and using a quiet, predetermined phrase to warn the others that the time has come to round off their stillness. It is important to allow a few extra moments for people to gather together their mental energies, which have been in abeyance for a while. These last few moments can also be used to reinforce whatever it is that has been found in the stillness, or to bring to mind any resolution or insight that has come out of the silence. It's good to remember that all is gift, and an acknowledgement of this by using head or hands is gentle and graceful. Sometimes it is fitting to stand in a circle and slowly repeat the Lord's Prayer or the Grace together, perhaps joining hands in shared thanksgiving.

METHOD: MEANINGLESSNESS OR MEANING?

Teachers of some of these methods insist that it is the method that is all: that the central point of stillness can be met devoid of all meaning; that it is the emptying itself which is of value in doing the exercise. Others would say that indeed the emptying can be of great value, but its value is much greater when it is refilled from an outside source of power and creativity. More than that, some teachers of meditation have discovered that to spend too long, too consistently, in an area of 'emptiness' carries grave risks with it. The prolonged emptiness can lead to a state of detached aloofness, a position of distancing from reality that is not simply being unstressed but is actually anti-social. Worse, prolonged emptiness may lead to the swept room being taken over by darker forces that bring spiritual confusion and the opposite of personal growth. It must be emphasized that whenever centering is sought in the company of God who is the source of love and peace and goodwill, these qualities will saturate the silence.

The grace and balance to be found within stillness cannot be forced or hurried. A correspondent expressed it like this:

> It's not what I do, but what is being done to me and in me that matters. It's so difficult to divest ourselves of the idea that we are central to the issue. We're not . . .

Her next words highlight the difference between methods and meanings.

> . . . we are just little 'us' facing the great 'All'. I just reach out to

God, let him clear the clutter. I know for certain it is no use agitating, with or without words, no use nagging him for the grace to be allowed nearer and deeper. I am in the stillness only to offer . . . not for what happens to my mind or my soul. He is the centre; the simple recognition of that is the first step, the whole journey, the end-goal and the end-product.

Personally, I never fail to be moved by how eagerly ordinary people take to silence, if only they are given a reasonably confident lead. There are myriad ways of using that space, but however many descriptions of 'what happens' are given, and however many 'techniques' are discovered, the basic mystery remains inexhaustible.

NOTES

[1]de Mello, Anthony, *Song of the Bird.* New York, Image Books, 1984 (p. 10).

[2]Those who explore this particular space in the silence would do well to have someone they trust alongside them.

[3]Those readers who are concerned that meditation and the use of the mantra are too strongly associated with New Age spirituality may be interested to know that a training package titled 'Christ-owned Relaxation and Stillness' is now being disseminated. Details from the author at C.O.R.S., 50B Hyde St., Winchester, Hants., SO23 7DY.

[4]op. cit., p. 98.

Chapter 7
CHILDREN AND STILLNESS

Children and stillness — a total contradiction in terms?

A reader wrote to a family journal recently, describing her experience as a four-year-old: 'I had an old trunk in the corner of a landing,' she says, 'where I would go just to sit and think. It was called my peace corner, and everyone in the family knew what it was. I went to it to be on my own.'

Maybe some people find the ideas of children and stillness incompatible; if they are convinced that children cannot, or will not, be silent, a few selected examples of published anecdotes may help.

YOUNG PEOPLE SILENCED!

' "Silence is golden" goes the saying, and so it was for about 25 young people who met for a silent retreat before their Confirmation.

The young people gathered together early on Friday evening and were silent from then on until after the service on Saturday morning.

Parents bringing food for the evening were surprised and most impressed to see their children refusing to break their silence and communicating with them using only signs.' (Extract from a newspaper in Fiji, South Pacific Islands)

'My way of praying is just praying with an open heart to him so that I get the open answer back.' (An eleven-year-old patient in Helen House, Oxford)[1]

From a teachers' manual of 'Stilling' exercises designed to be included in the National Curriculum comes this quotation from a fourteen-year-old girl: 'The point of stilling is to relax parts of our body and let them rest; to rest our minds and concentrate deeply on one activity; to blank our worries out so that we settle down and are at ease with our minds and bodies. It helps to feel our existence internally as well as externally'; and from a sixteen-year-old boy: 'The most helpful thing about the course was the stilling exercise. It made me happy whatever was going on, good or bad; it made me feel as if I wanted to help people. One thing I will remember about this course is the friendship we had together.'[2]

From a survey of 820 fifteen-year-olds in Britain, a number of joys and concerns were expressed that were basic to their needs. Among these was the desire to 'be oneself'.[3]

A teacher was told by a young boy at school: 'Everywhere is so busy, I have had to find eight separate secret places just so I can be sure of one when I need to be on my own.' And a secondary school boy told his mother: 'If only I could sometimes get away from the noise and the energy, just somewhere quiet so I could catch up on my own thoughts, then I would be alright . . .'[4]

I sat down in the park, alone,
For peace and quiet on my own,
But then some noisy children came,
Screaming, shouting — almost insane,
Until at last I could not bear to hear them shouting everywhere.

(Caroline Astley, aged 11 years)[5]

'The exterior silence did help us to feel more peaceful, to slow down a little, to be less breathless, but, like adults, *children thirst for inner silence* . . . Focusing total attention on a picture, a feather, a stone, a word, can be a means of stilling and quietening one's self so that it is possible to find one's inner self without too much turmoil. Once children have reached this, they are usually very keen to do it again. They ask if they can have meditation and refer to experiences they have had of being totally absorbed within themselves.'[6]

'That is my quiet place, where you can go if you're sad or annoyed. I like to go when no one is there, and there is a deathly silence, except for my breathing. Just you, God, and the silence.' (A ten-year-old)

What do we, as adults, *really* want for our children?

Contentment? which is contain-ment:
Balance? which is something held, on and at, a focal pivot:
Integrity? which is something that is whole, undivided, a thing complete in itself:
Confidence? which is with faith, self-assured, holding one's own.

If we want containment, balance, wholeness, assuredness, for our children, how is it that we have become so bad at letting them rediscover these things?

By nature children are born with a sense of contentment deep within them – once a baby is fed and warm, safe and comfortable, it will lie contentedly playing with its toes and watching the world go by until the next physical need makes itself felt. Gradually the series of needs grows more complex, and there comes a stage when the baby has to strive to get whatever it hasn't got. Then its basic contentment has to be stretched to include new goals. What could be a gentle development process is often 'improved' by adults who jump in and add to these efforts with continual stimulation and goading. Arousal and stimulation are important and exciting and necessary for the growing child, but if they are imposed too much, overload results in dissatisfaction, and contentment gets thrown out the window. The sad thing is that this demonstrates *our* discontent with our lot, rather than any original discontent in the child.

Consider, just for a moment, the following common incidents:

A baby a few months old lies cooing in its cot, playing contentedly with its toes. An adult comes in and covers the baby up, tucking its toes tightly inside.

A four-year-old is standing rapt by the dew sparkling on a spider's web. An adult comes up and takes the opportunity to interrupt the silence and fill the child's head with facts about the number of legs on a spider.

A six-year-old is engrossed in a single fascination – concentrated, un-hasty, unanxious, centred in the here and now. An adult comes out with 'put it away, it's time for tea'.

A nine-year-old who is clear-sighted, confident, unsceptical, is flying a kite. An adult rushes over with 'don't get cold, don't get muddy, don't fall over'.

No wonder children learn so well that to enjoy just being themselves, being on their own, is not to be done. Too often it is something that is not acceptable to adults.

'THE ORIGINAL VISION'[7]

Children are said to be closer in contact with their natural intuitions and centredness than older, more conditioned, adults. There has been considerable discussion of the meaning of 'centredness'[8] – that state of knowing something from the centre, intuitively. We cannot explain how we know it, but we just feel sure about it. Everyone has intuition, but some people have learned to use it more than others. Intuition is independent of the ways of knowing that we are familiar with, ways connected with our reasoning and our physical senses: it is an unaggressive sense of certainty, of knowing that you know something. It is different to knowing *about* something, it is knowing it as if it were part of you. It suddenly appears and brings with it a sense of clarity, and the feeling that the experience is 'right', at least for you. People say that they give their gut reactions attention in a sort of non-judgemental way, and then a strangely appropriate and unexpected insight arrives that seems to be more immediate than 'mere' reason. We were all born with this ability, and the ability to be centered; these things are in all of us somewhere.

BUT WHAT HAPPENS TO IT?

Some children reach into this deep fund of certainty easily, and they delight us adults with what we call their 'funny sayings'. It is often the children who daydream who have this sort of disarming naturalness. They will suddenly come out with ideas that seem to be gut hunches, 'rising from the belly'. And then equally easily we step in and trivialize their words with a puzzled and embarrassed response. We make a joke of it to our friends. We can't quite believe they can get so near the mark when they are so inexperienced and 'without knowledge'.

Of course sometimes the spontaneity of children has to be curbed so that they learn to fit in with other people; it has to be made 'reasonable' and 'sensible'. But as adults we can be too eager to impose our knowledge on them, and we fall into the trap of squashing their intuitiveness altogether. In time, the whole anabolic layer of experience (described in Chapter 2) is devalued and overridden until it is submerged altogether. In its place we put spoon-fed information and predigested excitements at such a rate that the children complain of being bored if they are missing. Eventually the young become so used to this constant external stimulation that it becomes a habit, almost an addiction, and it is because their own interior satisfactions have been disallowed — by us!! — and have atrophied.

Allowing young children the space to be, to mentally meander, to remain unquestioned and unquestioning for a while, reinforces this inner centredness, and shows that we value it. At times 'meditation' can be supervised and channelled in a deliberate fashion with a set place and time;[9] this sort of exercise suits some children and can bring great benefit. It should not be for too long; limiting the session to five minutes at the start will avoid the sort of resistance that can build up if something is pushed too hard from the outside. Let it develop naturally. In general though the most important thing is that adults should be seen to encourage the idea that 'it's O.K. to be still'. It has been said that adults need the single-mindedness of children. All we can achieve with our prized activity and doing is a sort of 'mental dizziness'.[10]

ADULT RESPONSIBILITY

Gradually, professionals are becoming aware of some of the dangers inherent in constantly urging children into activity and stimulation, achievement and competition. When parents, school staff, peers, commercial pressures, and the media all work at exciting young children, the time comes when their inborn contentment wears thin and they become intolerant of any gaps in their stimulation and need for instant satisfaction. Their inner experience is then about tension, demand, and incoherence; and they come to realize that the demand can *never* be filled because it is continually extended. This hyper-excitability means that any delay or frustration, inconvenience or uncertainty has to be covered over, masked, with more and more noise and activity. Experience has shown that when children are genuinely offered a safe way of retrieving personal space and inner stillness, they take to it as ducks take to water. It's like a homecoming.

At last it came to the end of a course of ten two-hour sessions during which a whole variety of social and coping skills had been introduced to a large group of fifteen-year-olds. There had been a lot of participation and each individual had been deeply involved in the discussions. The course had been held indoors out of necessity, although it was a brilliant summer and the bees had been buzzing on the inside of the window panes. The group was asked which skill they had enjoyed most, in spite of the heat and the distraction. One skill was voted for nine times more than any other. It was the practice of relaxation and stillness.

Where adults actually allow children the space to 'be', where they replace 'don't just sit there, do something' with just letting be, the response can be astonishing. They can experience the truth that we are human beings in spite of our constant human doings.

THE GAINS

There are other benefits – at all ages – from regaining a sense of centre:

- superficial conflicts become less absorbing, they lose their importance and their appeal;
- making decisions becomes easier, because what 'fits' is both more available and more obvious;
- trust in positive ways of living becomes more natural, and it also demands less effort;
- the strains, stresses, and strivings of ordinary life get put into a better sense of proportion;
- acceptance of myself as I am seems easier;
- all the non-rational faculties of intuition, creativity, reflection, being, are reinforced and new connections can be made between them and normal activity;
- laughter and playfulness come bubbling up with real spontaneous delight;
- most of all, the practice of regular centering enables children to get in touch with whatever it is that motivates them, and whatever it is that is true for them, as individual people.

HOW?

Once the need, the urgent need for children to recover their central stillness is acknowledged, there remains the adult disbelief of 'Yes, but *how?*' The immediate answer seems too simple – do it yourself, value it yourself, and the children will recognize it and claim it for themselves. There is no doubt that children take their clues from *us*, and if they don't see for themselves that we put a high priority on the use of silence and centering, they won't keep up its practice either. So underlying all the following ideas is the principle that stillness is something of visible importance to the adult who is supporting the child.

Suggested guidelines

From infancy

Just handling a new baby contentedly, in a way that is contained, being confident of *their* centredness; letting them be who they are, warmly, acceptingly. Sometimes it is quite difficult to resist the popular habit of rocking a baby over-energetically (which actually relates to our own anxiety), or of patting and petting the baby in a way which demands an active response (why do we, as adults, need such constant reassurance from the baby?). Sitting quietly nearby, enjoying the nearness of the new little person, and yet not being disturbed by its separateness is often preferable. Knowing that God holds us both in his hands.

The amazing self-possession of some very young babies and infants is wonderful; before any of our prized education, they seem to know who they are, that they are loved and whole, that their world is an alright place to be. The longer we can put off their disillusionment by demanding too much of them, the stronger this sense of being is likely to remain.

In toddlerhood

Simply being with, without constant intrusion into, the growing person's own perceptions. Keeping trust that those understandings will expand, at their own rate, and will select their own messages, without continual nagging and reinterpretation from us. Watching beautiful and absorbing things together, without words. Let them look and watch, listen and hear, and leave any discussion about it until later.

Sometimes it is good to let the toddler *see* the adult in a position of stillness. If the child comes into the room where an adult is meditating for instance, as likely as not the toddler will want to 'join in' and sit quietly alongside too.

When adults want to be quiet together and on their own, let them make it known among the children as something to be respected and valued. Some people just leave the door ajar so the child does not feel cut out, and perhaps can peep in and make sure the adults really are keeping still and quiet. The children will follow suit, and make up their own use of quietness. Take care to keep the silence anxiety-free, strong and convinced.

A young mother was washing up by the kitchen window on a beautiful spring morning. She was revelling in the sight of her glowing tulips, given to her on her wedding anniversary last year and flowering for the first time. The back door was open and she suddenly became aware that her toddler was making his way outside, lurching towards the best tulip. 'He'll grab it and crush it — he can't understand', and she rushed out to save the plant. As she approached him, her son was bent down over the brilliant flower, hand outstretched. She reached out to stop him as she heard him say, as he stroked the petals, 'Well done God, well done'.

With young schoolchildren

Reading together quietly, arms loosely round each other, listening to each other's viewpoint and not interrupting. Respecting what the other feels about things. Listening together[11] for short lengths of time (don't push it, accept that this is a very physical, active age) to birds, music, water and waves, someone singing next door, without *doing* anything about it. Avoid letting these times of mutual wordless enjoyment become strained or obligatory or selfconscious, but let them happen when they can — if necessary giving up something else that seems equally pressing — so the child knows his silent company is important to you. Just being alongside.

A teacher said that her class regularly practised stillness. She would put an hour-glass on a central table with a beautiful shell, or stone, or flower next to it; then the whole class would sit round it in perfect quietness, freed to do their own musing, while the glass slowly emptied from top to bottom. The stillness was never interrupted by the children.

A young grandmother and her grandchild who had just started school were climbing in the Lake District. They came across a small pond, high up in the hills, which had one perfect water-lily floating in the middle of it. 'Can we sit down?' asked the child, and the two of them settled at the edge of the water for a short rest. Forty-five minutes later, the child was still gazing at the water-lily, without any comment or interruption from the grandmother. Then, without preamble, very gradually and gently the child started to talk about the things that had been happening at school, the new feelings and strange situations. All the grandmother put in was an occasional 'Oh yes'; or 'I'm glad you told me that'.

In a little while the grandmother said 'Shall we move on?' and the child said, 'Let's look at the water-lily a bit longer first.'

When they finally returned to the bottom of the hill the child rushed over to her father with, 'Oh Daddy, we've had a lovely time. We've been watching a water-lily.' The grandmother pictured the scene as it might have been had the father been with them, with his keen interests; she imagined him saying, 'Yes, that's a water-lily alright, its Latin name is Nymphaea *and it's very rare in these parts. Let's go up higher and see how many more we can find, then we can go and tell the Warden all about it.'*

Three weeks later the grandmother had a letter from the grandchild. 'Thank you Granny for a lovely *holiday. I think of the water-lily every night before I go to sleep. Love, Jenny.'*

The older schoolchild

Accept that curiosity, activity, and belonging are preoccupations at this stage. Many children are over-extended by their own sense of adventure and their need to be seen as one of a group; they really have to be helped to 'calm down' in a way that is not always possible for them to do on their own. Unfortunately, all too frequently adults react to their seemingly boundless energy by shouting 'Calm down or I'll*** you'. Yet if a group is confidently given permission to be inactive, most children respond very positively especially if their feeling of 'what my friend does, I'll do' is built on. Watch the class as it flops down on the grass after physical activity at school – the children really make the most of the opportunity to let go and let up. In Sweden it is common practice for each class to start lessons with a brief session of exercise at their desks, followed by a few moments of sitting with heads resting on their arms. This practice is welcomed by the children, and their concentration during the lesson is greater. In Norway research is going on into the benefits of simple confidence-enhancing meditation for children who face class tests, and the results so far are remarkable. In England some teachers and school nurses are introducing informal methods of deep relaxation and visualization into classes, and it is a common experience for the children to ask for more. But it is usually the adults who have to allow the stilling.

In the face of these generalities, when a young boy was asked what he missed most at his boisterous weekly-boarding school he mumbled 'It's my cosy chair.' 'Your cosy chair?' the adult asked quietly. 'Yes,' as if apologetically, 'my cosy chair where I go when I want to curl up and be on my own. When I want to think things out for myself, that's what I miss.'

Adolescents

It's important to value their growing separateness, but to be ready and 'there' when they want to return. Talking gently and quietly together; it's not always important to cook up something impressive or trendy to say. You don't have to be there where they are all the time, but just be ready for them to share your centredness when they want to. And continue to let them know it is your priority even if it doesn't seem to be theirs; it will register and be remembered even if it is not often spoken about.

At the Greenbelt Arts Festival, 300 young people aged between 15 and 25 gathered together because they wanted to experience stillness. They chose to lie on the grass and become centered. However, it was by no means easy; in the marquee on their left was a brand new rock group which belted out enticing rhythms with the maximum volume at their command; in the marquee on their right was an evangelist who yelled at his audience enthusiastically, drawing out of them explosive roars of response. But 'Give us stillness' asked the 300 in the marquee in the middle. So they relaxed in silence and meditated upon 'Be still, and know that I am God'. There was not the smallest noise or least movement in the total stillness. The presence was powerful and pressing and the experience was unforgettable.

At all ages — IT'S O.K. TO BE STILL!!

And it's O.K. to be still separately. My centre is different from yours, and we don't own each other. We aren't images of each other. We are all different, separate, unique, and we each reflect a bit of the image of God. If it is validated, adolescents will develop their own areas of stillness. Adults — particularly family adults — mustn't translate it or possess it, direct, intrude or oversee it. Often they won't even know it's there.

The capacity for individuals to become opened to the creation and the Creator and bask there, without words and without demands, is vast. It was an anonymous teenager who said: 'Sometimes it is hard to explain . . . It is as if my inner-self is healing me and giving me a new perspective. I don't know, I can't explain it; you have to experience it for yourself. Maybe it is God or a part of God in me, just as it is in everyone else, but you have to find it.'[12]

This is quoted in a research report on *Religion and Values at Sixteen Plus* and its conclusion goes like this: 'In this superficially secularized culture of ours the word AIMS too often seems to stand for what might be called an Acquired Immunity to Mystery Syndrome — a condition that can well prove fatal to any spiritual growth. Yet here in these findings of ours we can see that the sense of mystery is far from dead among the young; that the 'original vision' which is the common birthright of us all has not yet faded beyond recovery' (p. 75).

Which is simply a modern way of saying what Wordsworth observed a long time ago –

> The Soul . . . cometh from afar:
> Not in entire forgetfulness,
> And not in utter nakedness,
> But trailing clouds of glory do we come . . .
> Heaven lies about us in our infancy! . . .
> The homely Nurse doth all she can
> To make her . . . child
> Forget the glories he hath known . . .
> A Presence that is not to be put by . . .
> . . . those first affections,
> Those shadowy recollections . . .
> Are yet the fountain-light of all our day . . .
> Uphold us, cherish, and have power to make
> Our noisy years seem moments in the being
> Of the eternal Silence . . .
>
> (Selected lines from Wordsworth's *Ode, Intimations of Immortality*)

There are ways that are both verbal and non-verbal to share with our children the deep deep knowledge – the gut-knowing – that

> Yes, we are imperfect . . .
> Yes, we are inadequate. . . .
> Yes, the world is unfair . . .
> Yes, life is full of risk, of uncertainty, of insecurity, of pain,
> BUT WHATEVER HAPPENS
> GOD WILL BE THERE
> WAITING TO DELIGHT IN US . . .

And if God is for us, who can be against us?

NOTES

[1]Quoted in the report *Children in the Way* prepared for General Synod, January 1987.
[2]Beesley, M., *Stilling*. Salisbury Diocese 1989.
[3]Extract from Simmons, C., 'Life at 15' in *Education and Health*, May 1985.
[4]Quoted by Nash, W., in *Christian Family*, August 1988.
[5]Quoted in Hinton, D., ed., *Fresh Voices*. N.C.E.C.
[6]Cardwell, R., *Helping Children to Pray*. Grail Publications.
[7]Robinson, E., *The Original Vision*. Seabury Press 1984.
[8]Hendricks and Roberts, *The Second Centering Book*. N. Y., Prentice Hall Press, 1977.
[9]Wilson, J., *First Steps in Meditation for Young People*. London, James Clarke & Co. Ltd., 1957. Reprinted 1990.
[10]Brother Roger, from Taizé Community, France.
[11]Faber and Mazlish, *How to Talk So Kids Will Listen and Listen So Kids Will Talk*. N. Y., Avon Books, 1982.
[12]Robinson and Jackson, *Religion and Values at Sixteen Plus*. Oxford, Alistair Hardy Research Centre, 1987 (p. 17ff).

Part Two: THE TOOLS

The aim of this section of the book is to provide readers with actual tools to use. These tools will serve just as well if they are used for personal prayer in private, or if they are used in a group. The book has been bound in a way that allows it to open, flat, at a chosen page, either on a table or the floor, where the prayer(s) can see it comfortably. Whenever distractions seem to get in the way, it is then easy to make a gentle return to the theme of the silence by a glance at the spread page.

The contents of this section are in four parts:

1 **Lead-ins** These are particularly helpful when the time for silence has been preceded by some exercise or discussion or busyness. Each lead-in takes about 5 minutes. They are made up of sentences to be read slowly and quietly, with about 45 seconds of silence allowed between each, so that the next sentence drops quietly into the pool of growing concentration. Reduced lighting is helpful.

The four lead-ins outlined here are:

- the *Sarum Prayer*, which is good when a group wants to make a verbal response to the leader;
- texts of *Stillness*, which are particularly appreciated by those who want biblical references;
- the ladder of the *Senses*, which helps to encourage an awareness of the here and now;
- different methods of *Breathing*, with which to sink into quiet.

After the lead-in, the leader can say: 'While your bodies are still and relaxed, I offer you a picture on which to concentrate your mind.'

2 **Fantasy Imaging** These are imaginary pictures that can be used again and again and each time a different slant of insight seems to come. This use of the imagination makes it possible to get in touch with our own intuitions. If total silence is difficult to hold, the low-key, continuous train of thought suggested by these images is very rewarding.

The ones outlined here are:

- colours;
- the butterfly garden;
- scattering – gathering;
- replenishment.

3 **Symbol Meditations** These are useful both for focusing and for their meaning. They can be used with the appropriate object placed where it can be seen conveniently, or just by picturing the symbol in the mind. Those described here are:

- the towel;
- the candle;
- the goblet;
- the funnel.

4 **Using a Mantra** The use of one phrase or word as a means of focusing deeply has been in the traditions of Christianity and Eastern religions since they were first formed. A modern translation of Jesus' phrase 'he that hath ears, let him hear' is 'let it sink deeply into your ears', and this description cannot be bettered.

From St Augustine who wrote of this type of centering as 'the heart giving birth to something it cannot speak of', and again 'with your heart rejoicing without words, and the immense breadth of your joy not rationed out in syllables',[1] through the teachings of the author of *The Cloud of Unknowing*, John Cassian, St John of the Cross, St Teresa of Avila, to more modern scholars such as William Johnston, Basil Pennington, Arthur Slade and John Main, there is no lack of witnesses to the abundant experience opened up by this way of centering. A busy friend said to me: 'Words curb me. One word is like an entry to a whole new world of wordlessness, freed from the shackles of definitions. Wonder and mystery.'

It's rather like a quarry; each time I dig into it something different comes out. We are told that Jesus Christ himself used to play on words to increase their meaning. For instance, he used the one sound *ruach* to describe breath, and wind, and spirit;[2] and the 'eye of the needle' idea was used by him to describe both the difficulties of a laden camel passing through a narrow gate and someone loaded with riches passing through the gate of the kingdom of God.[3] Dame Julian certainly made the most use of 'punning' with words describing things of the spirit. She enjoyed playing with words like 'born' and 'borne'; 'kind' and 'kinde' (kindred); 'laws' and 'lores' to reinforce her meanings.[4] This play of layering words has been used here too, each word acting as a carrier for several overlays of meaning that reflect, or echo, or light up each other. There are many mantras, and they are each personal to the individuals who choose them; the ones I have included here have all got this in common – each one represents not one but several meanings. Readers will probably enjoy discovering others for themselves. Centering certainly doesn't have to be solemn; St Mechtilde in the fourteenth century said, God wants us as playmates!

Using a mantra frees one from the limits put on words of description; the mantras supplied here are *not* explained or 'drawn out' with more words; however they *are* 'drawn out' by a symbolic illustration. There are also biblical associations which reflect upon them. The more often each is used, the more use it becomes. Some teachers insist that one mantra should be repeated for an entire lifetime. The use of one word or sound enables one to hook into the one point that matters, below and above all other issues, all other concerns. It becomes the one tap-root, that focuses, anchors, and nourishes everything else in life; the one meaning that gives life to all other meanings.

Coming back It is important to allow enough time for each member of the group to come back to the noise and demand of social interaction without losing the stillness that has been gained. It must not be clumsily hurried, and may take several minutes. A good idea is to reclaim each of the faculties that have been lain aside. E.g. 'slowly, become aware of energy returning to your muscles . . . the sensation of touch returning to your fingers . . . the sense of hearing the small sounds in this room to your ears . . . and lastly, the sense of light to your eyes . . . when you are ready to rejoin the group, wriggle your fingers and open your eyes.'

The main hope which underlies all these offerings is that they may act as a gateway to an affirmation and relationship with the God who is beyond words, in a manner that is beyond words, and bring with them an 'in-filling' that is beyond words.

NOTES

[1] Quoted by Rowan Williams, p. 87. *The Wound of Knowledge*. London, Darton, Longman and Todd, 1981.

[2] Although some of the significance of these sayings is lost in their translation, *ruach* is used both to describe the strong wind/spirit/breath which brought the dry bones back to life in Ezekiel ch. 37, and in Christ's conversation with Nicodemus about the life of the Spirit (John 3:8).

[3] Matthew 19:24.

[4] Julian of Norwich, *Revelations*, c.f. ch. 51.

1:LEAD-INS

THE SARUM PRAYER

This form of preparation has been used down the centuries in a number of ways. As a lead-in to stillness it is obviously valuable to individuals, but it has a special benefit to groups since it is so familiar it binds the group together immediately, and it allows for group response where this is wanted. The 'leader' can be any member of the group, it certainly doesn't have to be the usual or acknowledged host. It is important that the person who takes it has the confidence to leave sufficient time in between the petitions for general 'settling' after each one. The total lead-in should take 5 or 6 minutes. Then, when all is still and uncluttered, it's time to introduce the theme of the silence.

Leader: God be in my head –
Group response: And in my understanding . . .
Aim for stillness in the mind. Let go of all the cares, anxieties, concerns, that came into the room with you. Put them all on one side, or into an imaginary box under your chair. They will wait there until you can attend to them again later. Feel your mind unwinding. Let its normal alertness become slack. Make mental space for God, let him take over.

Leader: God be in my eyes –
Group response: And in my looking . . .
Aim for quietness of the eyes. Let go of the sights, messages, worries, and delights that come in through the eyes. Give them to God. Leave behind all the clever thoughts that come to you by reading and looking, leave them under your chair – the important ones will still be there later, waiting for you to retrieve them. Make 'seeing' space for God.

Leader: God be in my ears –
Group response: And in my hearing . . .
Aim for quietness of the ears. Let go of all that irritating comment and annoying gossip that has been hanging around. Offer back to God any words about your own efforts that you prize. Leave the outside noises outside.

Leader: God be in my mouth –
Group response: And in my speaking . . .
Aim for stillness of the tongue. Let go of all the normal tension in the throat, cheeks, soft palate, tongue – all the muscles used for speech and eating. Offer any regretted words to God. Let them go . . .

Leader: God be in my heart –
Group response: And in my feelings . . .
Aim for quietness in the heart. Panics and fears and doubts, let them go. Strong passions of all sorts, good and bad, positive and negative, put them away for now. They are just a distraction at the moment, and God will hold them in his peace until you own them again later.

Leader: God be at my ends –
Group response: And in my departings . . .
'Ends' can be beginnings or departings, they are all important but look for total stillness just now. Peace at starting, continuing, completing; peace always, all ways, all times. Stillness at the centre, now.

BIBLICAL TEXTS OF STILLNESS

First level of stillness: our EMOTIONAL self;
For this present moment, think of stilling all strong feelings; detach from them, put them on one side, to be attended to later.

Commune with thy heart . . . and be still. (Psalm 4:4)

Second level of stillness: our PHYSICAL self;
Take up a good sitting posture: bottom well back into the seat of the chair, back upright, knees uncrossed, hands resting loosely open on your lap, feet flat on the floor.
Think of relaxing all body muscles, quieten all movement and speech.

Their strength . . . is to sit still. (Isaiah 30:7)

Third level of stillness: our MENTAL, INTELLECTUAL self;
Still all the questioning, debating, doubting, that constantly occupies your mind. Quieten the reasoning, leave that to another time.

Only be silent . . . and let silence be your wisdom. (Job 13:5, *NEB*)

Fourth level of stillness: our SPIRITUAL self;
Stop, for a while, all your efforts to prove how good you are, still all your attempts to earn God's approval – it can't be earned. Be content to Be, to be held, to be known; just as you are.

Be still . . . and know . . . that I am . . . God. (Psalm 46:10)

Other alternatives, for different occasions:

Peace . . . be still. (Mark 4:39)

Return to thy stillness, O my Soul, for the Lord hath dealt bountifully with thee. (Psalm 116:7)

In returning . . . rest . . . quietness . . . and confidence, shall be thy strength. (Isaiah 30:15)

THE LADDER OF THE SENSES

This is an exercise of becoming aware of ourselves, in order to open ourselves up to God at the centre. The following is laid out as for use with a group, but it is easy enough to replace the words of 'we', 'us', and 'our', with 'I', 'me', and 'my'.

We have been moving about, using our bodies to respond to each other and to take part in the world around us, and that has been good and enjoyable;
but for now, we put all movement on one side, ***in order to take part in the stillness that is inside.***

(Pause for at least 1 minute.)

We have been talking, making contact with each other and exchanging ideas, and that has been good and enjoyable;
but for now, we put that exchange on one side, we still our tongues and our words, ***in order to make contact with the stillness that is inside.***

(Pause for at least 1 minute.)

We have been tasting our food, savouring its flavours, and that has been good and enjoyable;
but for now, we put all savouring and judging on one side, ***in order to taste the stillness that is inside.***

(Pause for at least 1 minute.)

We have been using our eyes to see, to send and to receive messages from each other, to get in touch, and that has been good and enjoyable;
but for now, we put our outside seeing on one side, ***in order to get in touch with the insight that is inside.***

(Pause for at least 1 minute.)

We have been using our ears to listen to sounds around us, and to hear what others have been saying, and that has been good and enjoyable;
but for now, we put our outside hearing on one side, **in order to listen to our centre, where God lives, on the inside.**

(Pause for at least 1 minute, then lead into the theme or the mantra.)

ANABOLIC BREATHING

Ana = Greek root for up, again, anew . . .
Catabolic – striving for what I am not yet . . .
resources wearing Down;
Anabolic – content, for this moment, to be where I am now . . .
resources renewed, building Up. (See Chapter 2.)

Anabolic breathing, using the abdominal muscles and diaphragm, stimulates the *parasympathetic* nervous system: i.e. the physiological responses that are the converse of classical 'stress' responses.

Method

(a) Think of your head, and all the busy thoughts going around in your mind. Think of the rather fast, high-up 'head' breathing that goes with busyness, the sort of breathing that singers use when they are reaching for the top notes . . .
Now deliberately still your mind, calm the busyness, quieten that straining; and notice how your breathing gets calmer and lower . . . your breathing gets lower down into your chest . . .

(b) Your heart is in your chest: traditionally, your heart is the focus of a lot of emotions; think of how you breathe when you are feeling emotional, it is said your chest heaves up and down, great sighs make your chest muscles work hard . . .
Now deliberately calm your chest-breathing muscles . . . quieten your emotions down . . . still your heart and your feelings . . . and notice your centre of breathing gets lower . . . it goes lower, it centres down lower in your abdomen . . .

(c) Your abdomen and lower trunk house all the biggest muscles in your body, a lot of important physical functions are in this area; the strong muscles of the abdominal wall, the strong muscles you sit on, the strong muscles of the thighs . . .
Now deliberately calm those muscles . . . quieten the movements they make . . . still those functions . . . let your tummy be softly rounded as you breath in . . . lowered as you breathe out . . . your chest walls are not moving at all, all your breathing is done low down in your body . . . low down . . . lower and lower . . .

IT'S AS IF YOU ARE REACHING THE GROUND OF YOUR BEING . . .
Resting in the ground of your being . . . the ground of your being is where God is. Rest there, relaxed and trusting . . . He is supporting you on the ground . . . He made the ground . . . He is the ground . . . the ground of your being . . .

When it is time, give thanks for the strength that is in the ground, for that assurance, that security . . . But for now, gather some energy from the ground back into your body . . . Bring some of the assurance, that strength, back with you, back up your legs, back up your trunk, shoulders, arms . . . you know you can find that ground of being again at any time, whenever you want to . . . wriggle your fingers . . . and prepare to rejoin the group.

2:FANTASY IMAGING

The following four examples of fantasy images are most effective when they are used following one of the previous lead-ins and when those present are deeply relaxed but perhaps as yet are unfamiliar with complete silence. They should be read by a leader in a low voice, very slowly and calmly, as if telling a quiet story. Take about 10–15 minutes to complete the image. If participants later say they got 'lost' and 'didn't hear it all', that is all to the good!

COLOURS

With your eyes gently closed, imagine the first crocus of spring. It has been an icy winter, and the earth is hard. One brave spear has pierced the ground and you can see one tiny spot of yellow — *bright courageous yellow*. Concentrate on that tiny spot of *courageous* yellow.

The year moves on and the crocus gives place to a small bed of tulips. They are bright and close, making a patch of *brilliant cheerful red*. Concentrate on that small patch of *cheerful* red tulips.

The year moves on and the patch of tulips gives way to a large meadow of new corn; it's a *fertile creative green*. Concentrate on that large area of fertile *creative* green.

The year moves on. It's high summer, and the meadow reaches down to the sea. In front of you, as far as your eye can see, there stretches a *vastness of the purest blue*. Concentrate on that sea of *purest* blue.

And now night has fallen over the sea and there is a tropical night sky. Around you and over you as far as the sky can go there is *deep purple peace*. Let that deep profound peace surround you. Lose yourself in that deep purple peace, concentrate only on that encompassing purple *peace*. God's peace.

That deep peace of God is always there; you can come back to it whenever you want to; it is always there to be found. But for now, keep a bit in your heart, and when you are ready . . .

in your own good time . . .
gently and slowly . . .
prepare to rejoin the group, bringing back some
of that sense of the peace of God with you.

THE BUTTERFLY GARDEN

It is a glorious afternoon: the sun is shining brightly from a clear blue sky. A soft breeze makes the air balmy, and stops the heat from being too overbearing.

I'm sitting in a small enclosed garden, on my own, enjoying the smell of the newly cut green grass, the scents of the flowers, the shapes of the various shrubs.

There are masses of differently coloured butterflies around the garden: all shapes and sizes; look at the intricacy of the patterns on their wings! Their beauty and gentleness! The movement and colour!

One very special one settles down just near where I am: concentrate on that one. Very still, don't disturb it. Watch closely, silently, not stirring.

The one butterfly senses the stillness, soon its antennae stop quivering. It senses the warmth of the sun on its back, rests its wings, stays softly where it is, basking.

Look closely, closely, at the one butterfly; look at the dark pattern on its back, look at the centre of its spread wings — is there a cross in that pattern?

Concentrate on the centre of that cross. Is there one word there, right over the heart of the butterfly? What is that word? It is enfolded when the butterfly closes its wings.

The butterfly is settled; warm, safe, contained.

What was that word? Hold onto that word; hold it, enfold it, be enfolded by it. Stay there as long as it is comfortable, not thinking, not doing, just sitting and being.

That sense of safe containment is always there; you can come back to it whenever you want to; it is always there ready to be found. But for now, just keep a bit of it in your heart, when you are ready . . .

in your own good time . . .
gently and slowly . . .
prepare to rejoin the group, bringing some of that sense of safe containment with you.

SCATTERING—GATHERING?

Walk into your own small private room and close the door quietly behind you. It's warm and velvety-brown dark in your room; sit down in one of the comfortable chairs and just get accustomed to the quiet and peace.

On one wall of your room there is a screen, and you notice a picture coming up on it. It is the image of a large daisy-like flower, perhaps the enlargement of a single white marguerite.

Notice how open it is, the petals wide-spread; the petals are broad, each one easy to hold between a thumb and finger.

Watch . . . two young children come and look at your flower . . . one of them plays the old game with it, pulling out one petal at a time — 'he loves me, he loves me not' . . . Soon only the centre of the flower is left, bereft, and the children fade out of the picture.

Now there is another flower, a fresh marguerite, on your screen. Get into the flower: it's you, *be* that flower. You are fresh, and white, and whole.

Each time you do something, or give away a part of yourself, a petal drops off. Look at the scattered petals, each one a part of you you have given away . . . the heart of the flower, the centre, is in danger of being left bare. (*Don't pause too long here.*)

My petals have been important as a means of getting pollen to the centre of my flower, it's there that the seeds mature and where the fruit grows.

When the pollen has been gathered into the centre of the flower, then the fruit will grow in spite of the petals becoming scattered.

Have I been 'scattered'?

Or have I made sure the petals produced a gathering of pollen, so the centre will mature and seeds will grow?

Scattering and gathering . . . Scattering and gathering . . . Scattering and gathering . . .

Centre now; whatever my faults, my gaps, my inadequacies, my mistakes, there's always a new start offered by the Creator. Becoming centred, rooted, grounded, established, in him; and he in me.

He is always there, always the Ground of my Being, always there to be returned to, always ready to gather me . . .

Slowly and gently, the picture on the screen fades . . . I get up out of my comfortable brown chair . . . I walk to the door of my private room . . . open it quietly and close it firmly behind me . . . Having been gathered. . . . I can now return . . . gently . . . to the group.

REPLENISHMENT

This is a daydream, and in a daydream anything can happen!

Use your imagination:

You are in a small boat, a dinghy, on a stretch of water.

- For some time you have been preoccupied with the oars, working hard at getting to wherever it is you want to go.
- It's tough work, because the paddles are small and not particularly efficient, and you don't feel particularly strong. You know you are not cut out to be a long-distance rower.
- It gets hotter; you get hotter; you're getting fed-up and tired and above all, thirsty.
  Hot and bothered; tired and thirsty.
- Nothing in the boat but a ladle . . . that's not much good because you can't drink salt water.
- Bit desperate by now . . . nearly at the end of your tether . . . give it a go and *try it out – dip the ladle in the water . . .*
- *It's clear and fresh*!!! You're on a fresh water lake, not on the sea!
- The water you're drinking is fed by underground springs, you can drink it to your heart's content!
- You are refreshed, replenished, filled with new energy to complete your journey . . . What is the name of the water that replenished you?

What is the name of your water? Keep that name close to your heart.

Stay with it, the relief, the delight, the refreshment, the gratitude. Hold it in the silence for as long as it takes.

You can come back to be replenished, infilled, any time you want to, it will always be there. Keep the name of it close to you, and bring some of it back with you, when just for now . . .

when you are ready . . .
in your own good time . . .
gently and slowly . . . draw back some energy into your body, your arms, your fingers, and prepare to rejoin the group.

3:SYMBOL MEDITATIONS

A TOWEL

(1) I'm looking at a towel; it's an attractive towel, I like the colour and the design of it.

(2) Most of the time this towel spends its life neatly folded . . . stored in a tidy hot-cupboard. It feels warm and clean and safe in there, but it's not really much use to anybody.

(3) The towel is only really *useful* when it is taken out into the cold world and opened up, and spread out, and wrapped around someone — someone who is uncomfortable because they are wet. Then it absorbs all the wet . . . it makes no fuss when it is left a bit damp itself.

(4) The person who has used the towel to soak up all the wet isn't necessarily grateful; as often as not it is left in a heap on the floor, and perhaps it gets dirty too.

(5) Then there is the turmoil of the washing machine — it's tumbled around and twisted and gets knotted up. The movement, the noise, the commotion. The busyness.

(6) And then, at last, it can get out into the sun. Stretched out to its fullest extent, but not being used, not doing anything, just basking in the light and the warmth and the radiance of the sun. Just being . . .

That's what my towel really likes, that's what makes life worth living.

Now, go through the six steps of the meditation again, but this time it's not just an objective towel; this time *you* are the towel.

(1) .... (2) ....
(3) .... (4) ....
(5) .... (6) ....
Stay there for as long as is comfortable ....Feel better now?

THE CANDLE

Where feasible, light a candle and place it below the eye level of whatever position you are taking. Make any other lighting dimmer.

The candle is small, it is neither important nor powerful . . .

But it is warm, and beautiful . . .

Its use is well tried; it has been loved down the centuries by those who want to lighten their way . . . to learn . . . to worship . . . to love.

Put it in a dark room, and the darkness retreats, the whole room is made lighter.

However dark the dark may be, the candle is never overcome by dark.

It stands firmly on its base, upright, always reaching upwards.

The flame waves and dips, dancing in the currents of air . . . but the base remains secure and stable, unmoved by the movements of the flame.

The wick appears to be on fire, but it is not itself destroyed while it can glow on the melted wax, the gift of the candle.

The flame always reaches upwards; when it dips it always comes back to reaching upwards . . . it never sways for too long.

I am a candle . . . How much of this applies to me? . . .

THE GOBLET

On the table just near me is a goblet. It is not a valuable or rare goblet, but because it is ceramic and handmade it is totally unique; there is no other goblet in the world identical to this goblet. So it is precious for its uniqueness. Like me.

The goblet has a round flat base which keeps it securely on the ground.

But the upper part resembles two hands, little fingers and thumbs held together, while the palms form a cup and all the finger tips are opened to receive whatever is poured into it.

As long as it is reaching upwards, the goblet can be filled.

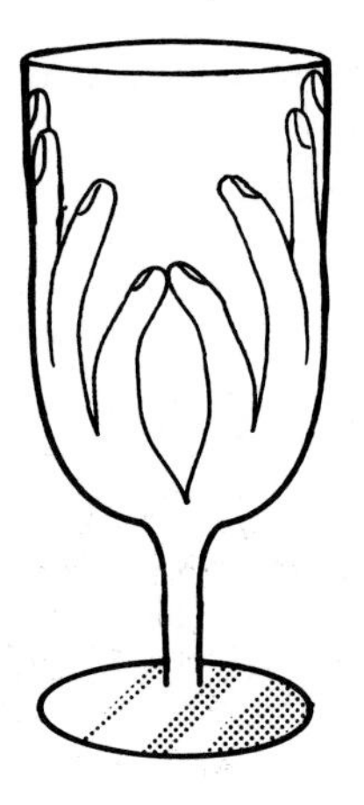

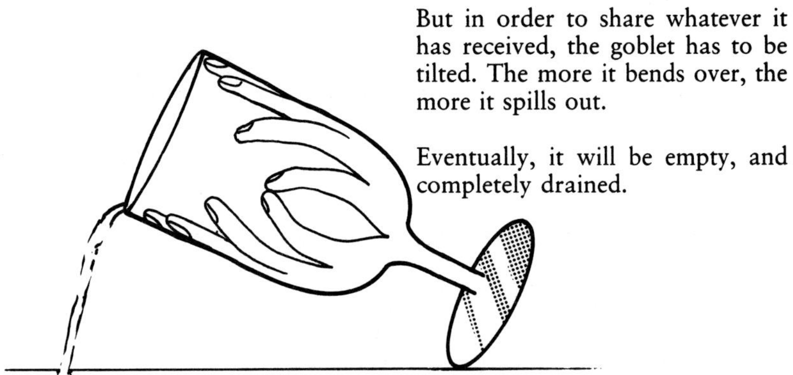

But in order to share whatever it has received, the goblet has to be tilted. The more it bends over, the more it spills out.

Eventually, it will be empty, and completely drained.

And then, in order to be refilled, the goblet must return to the upright. It must stand still on its secure base and accept whatever it is that fills it up.

What refills me? Can I share it with others?

THE FUNNEL

(First, the observations.)
In front of me is a funnel. It is a very ordinary, plastic, domestic funnel, nothing out-of-the-way, or 'fancy', no special decoration.

It's an object that is in everyday use, and it is superbly suited to its function.

The funnel can't stand on its own: it's supported by a tripod.

This funnel has a wide open outer edge . . . it has no control over what is poured into it . . .

The function of the funnel is to receive whatever comes in . . .

The funnel has no lid, so nothing is stopped from coming in . . . nothing is rejected . . . nothing is blocked . . .

The funnel has no plug, so nothing is clung on to . . . everything flows . . . there is continuous flowing . . .

It accepts all that comes into it, but it does have some control over how the contents flow out . . .

They flow out in a more directed stream, a more controlled stream . . .

(Then, the inferences.)
The funnel accepts all that comes to it. The funnel clings on to nothing, but lets it all *flow* through, so it doesn't get blocked, bogged down, or clogged up . . .

Is my life clogged, static? What is blocking it? Could I *flow* more, let go more, allow things through more?

Where do things go, when they pass from me? Have they been altered?

What supports *me*? What is the name of my tripod? Is it that of my family? my friends? my work? my pets? . . . the Trinity?

4:USING A MANTRA

It's always a good idea to take a few moments settling in physically, emotionally and mentally to the idea of being uninterrupted and still. Don't rush this preparation, whatever form it takes. Acknowledge each activity that has been your concern immediately beforehand — what you have been doing, what you have been feeling, and what you have been thinking; what has been worrying you, what you are pleased about, and what you are planning. Take hold of each of these things and quite deliberately put them on one side to wait until later for their due attention; their time will come but their time is not *now*. Use one of the lead-ins that you are comfortable with.

The following format can be said on one's own, or in a group. The words can be said out loud either by a leader, or (when it is familiar) in turn by members of the group, or just to yourself, vocalized or silently.

It is wonderful too, when you are lonely, or afraid, or lying awake.

So, to start off with, here is something very easy and very beautiful:

Behold . . . I am with you always . . . (2 minutes silence.)

Behold . . . I am with you **all ways** . . . (2 minutes silence.)

Behold . . . I am **with you** . . . (2 minutes silence.)

Behold . . . **I am** . . . (2 minutes silence.)

Behold . . . (2 minutes silence.)

Be . . . (Keep silence for as long as is comfortable.)

In Western society, the use of the mantra among ordinary people is far more widespread than might be supposed just by watching faces in the street. Any space of unthinking time can be used to focus on a mantra, and there are a great variety of sounds and words or phrases that can be used. Once a particular mantra has really been 'owned', it will spring to mind at any odd moment of the day, and bring with it the assurance and collectedness we all need. It supports the 'flow' between people, and lowers the need to be defensive. It reminds us constantly of the presence of God.

Sample mantras would include:

. . . Peace . . .
. . . Shalom . . .
. . . Maranatha . . .
. . . Yours . . .
. . . Amen . . .
. . . One . . .
. . . Glory to God, goodwill to mankind . . .

Examples of personalized mantras were sent to me by a correspondent. This lady uses a two-fold phrase, the first part being said with the in-breath, and the second being said with the out-breath. Sometimes the words can be repeated out loud, when there are a lot of distractions around, or they can be whispered to oneself, or just heard with the inner ear so the words rest on the heart. The phrases suggested are:

Being here (*in-breath*) . . . for God (*out-breath*)
or
All the doors . . . are open
or
God of all . . . Yes

There will be others that readers discover and make individual for themselves.

Then there is the centuries old 'Jesus Prayer':

Lord Jesus Christ . . . have mercy

The only important thing is that the words chosen should be wholly *right* for the user. Stillness of attention is not designed to 'achieve' anything, it simply re-links us with our centre of being, reconnects us to our true wholeness. In our frenetic and distracted world, this is a matter of urgency, when 'calmness will overcome chaos, and coolness will overcome heat'.[1]

There is a physiological technique for 'Stilling the mind' for those who find focusing difficult, which is expounded by Joe Macdonald Wallace in his book *Stress*.[2] It is based on the theory that whenever we 'think', we use minute movements of the muscles with which we verbalize (talk) and visualize (see). If we become aware of these small movements, we can take control of them and, with practice, still them. When the muscles themselves are totally still, we are no longer able to 'think'.

The theory can be tested in two ways: firstly for those who mainly think in words – verbalizers, and secondly for those who mainly think in pictures – visualizers.

1. Take time to mouth slowly, in a very exaggerated manner, a few lines of any nursery rhyme. While doing this, notice the feelings of stretch in the muscles of the tongue, cheeks, lips, throat, and palate. Repeat the chosen lines more quietly, and gradually lessen the movements of the speech muscles. Lastly have the lips closed, and keep all the muscles in the mouth totally still. When complete control is gained of the muscle movements, and they are completely still, the mind will be unable to 'talk'.
2. In a similar way, first become aware of the movements of the muscles surrounding the eye, the eyeball, and the eyelid. This can be done by making exaggerated movements with these muscles, and then, in stages, deliberately quietening them down. When total control of the muscle movement has been gained, and they are completely still, the mind will be unable to 'see'.

Thinking may be stopped only momentarily, but it will be enough to provide the clue to stillness in the mind.

At this point, a word of warning is in order. Kaplan puts it well:

> Mantra meditation can be dangerous for someone with a history of mental illness. If a person's connection to the real world is not strong to begin with, he may have difficulty re-establishing his connection with reality after a deep meditative experience. Just as certain forms of strenuous exercise must be avoided by people with a history of heart trouble, certain forms of mental exercise must be avoided by people with a history of mental illness. Any person with doubts about his mental stability should make sure he has an expert guide before becoming involved with any type of intense meditation.[3]

Some authorities suggest that Jesus Christ himself was familiar with the use of the mantra. Historically and geographically, the position of both the culture and the land that he was brought up in was closer to ancient spiritual traditions than we are. The long nights he spent praying to God his father would have included stretches of stillness, and perhaps his stay was the sound 'Abba'. The stripped, uncluttered, flow between the Father and the Son was the source of his spiritual power. Maybe we too can make our own attempts to emulate Christ. We can know that he will be accompanying us, if we go into silence in his name.

NOTES

[1]Quoted by Laurence Freeman OSB, *Benedictine Priory Newsletter*, 1990.
[2]Joe Macdonald Wallace, *Stress*. Crowood Press, 1988.
[3]Aryeh Kaplan, *Jewish Meditation*. New York, Schocken Books, 1985.

I AM – the earliest name of God

i am – describing myself (e.e. cummings)

iam – Latin for **NOW**

Bible references
Exodus 3:14 'And God said: *I AM that I AM . . .*'
Revelation 1:8 '*I am the Alpha and the Omega . . .*'
John 8:58 'Before Abraham ever was, I AM . . .'

Mark 14:62 'Are you the Christ? *I am . . .*'
John 6:35 'I am the bread of life . . .'
8:12 'I am the light of the world . . .'
10:7 'I am the gate of the sheepfold . . .'
10:11 'I am the good shepherd . . .'
11:25 'I am the resurrection and the life . . .'
14:6 'I am the way, the truth, and the life . . .'
15:5 'I am the vine, you are the branches . . .'
18:37 'Yes, I am a king . . .'
Acts 22:8 '*I am Jesus . . .*'

i am not sorry when silence becomes singing
winter by spring; i lift my diminutive spire to
merciful Him whose only now is forever:
standing erect in the deathless truth of His presence
welcoming humbly His light and proudly His darkness
(e.e. cummings, *selected poems 1923–1953*, Faber and Faber)

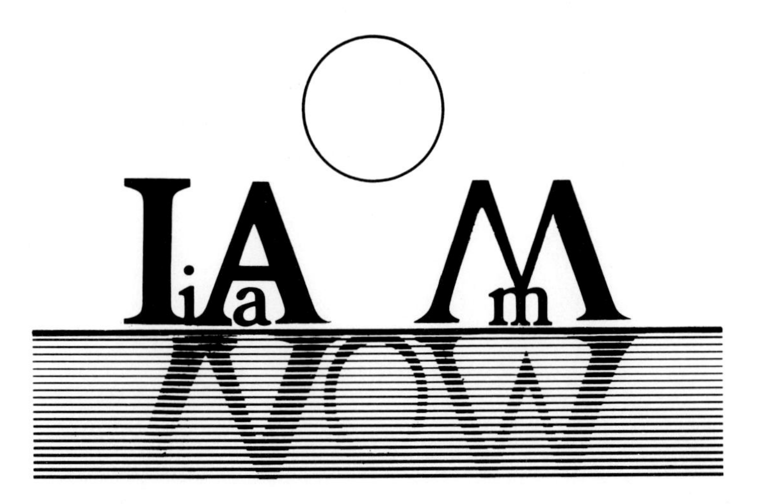
I A M
i a m

ASSENT
ASCENT:

Bible references

2 Chronicles 18:12 'The words of the prophets declare good to the king with one assent . . . even what my God saith, that will I speak.'

Acts 10:4 'Your offering of prayers ascended to speak for you to God.'

Psalm 139:8 'If I ascend up into heaven, thou art there;
If I make my bed in hell, behold, thou art there also.'

Revelation 11:12 'And they heard a great voice from heaven saying unto them, come up hither . . . and they ascended up to heaven.'

(saying 'Yes' to God
Lord, here I am, send me)

HOLY
WHOLE
HOLE
HOLED

(HOLY GOD
HOLD me
when I feel HOLED;
that I may be WHOLED into you)

at PEACE

or

in PIECES:

Bible references

1 Kings 19:11 ‘A strong wind brake in pieces the rocks before the Lord, but the Lord was not in the wind . . .’

Lamentations 3:11 ‘He hath turned aside my ways and pulled me in pieces: he hath made me desolate . . .’

Micah 3:2–3 ‘Who hate the good and love the evil; they break their bones and chop them in pieces . . .’

Luke 2:14 ‘Glory to God . . . and peace to men who enjoy his favour . . .’

John 14:27 ‘Peace I bequeath to you, my own peace I give you . . .

1 Corinthians 14:33 ‘God is not a God of disorder but of peace . . .’

Philippians 4:7 ‘The peace of God, which passes understanding . . .’

PRAYS
PRAISE:

Bible references

Acts 9:11 'Behold he prays . . .'

Psalm 55:17 'Evening, morning, and at noon will I pray . . .'

Romans 8:26 'We do not know how to pray worthily as sons of God, but his Spirit within us is actually praying for us in those agonizing longings which never find words. And God who knows the hearts' secrets understands, of course, the Spirit's intention as *he prays* for those who love God . . .' (J. B. Phillips translation.)

1 Thessalonians 5:17 'Pray without ceasing . . .'

Psalm 34:1 'His praise shall be continually in my mouth . . .'

Psalm 71:14 'I will yet praise thee more and more . . .'

Acts 2:46 'Continually in the temple, praising and blessing God . . .'

1 Peter 4:11 'Jesus Christ, to whom be praise and dominion for ever and ever, Amen.'

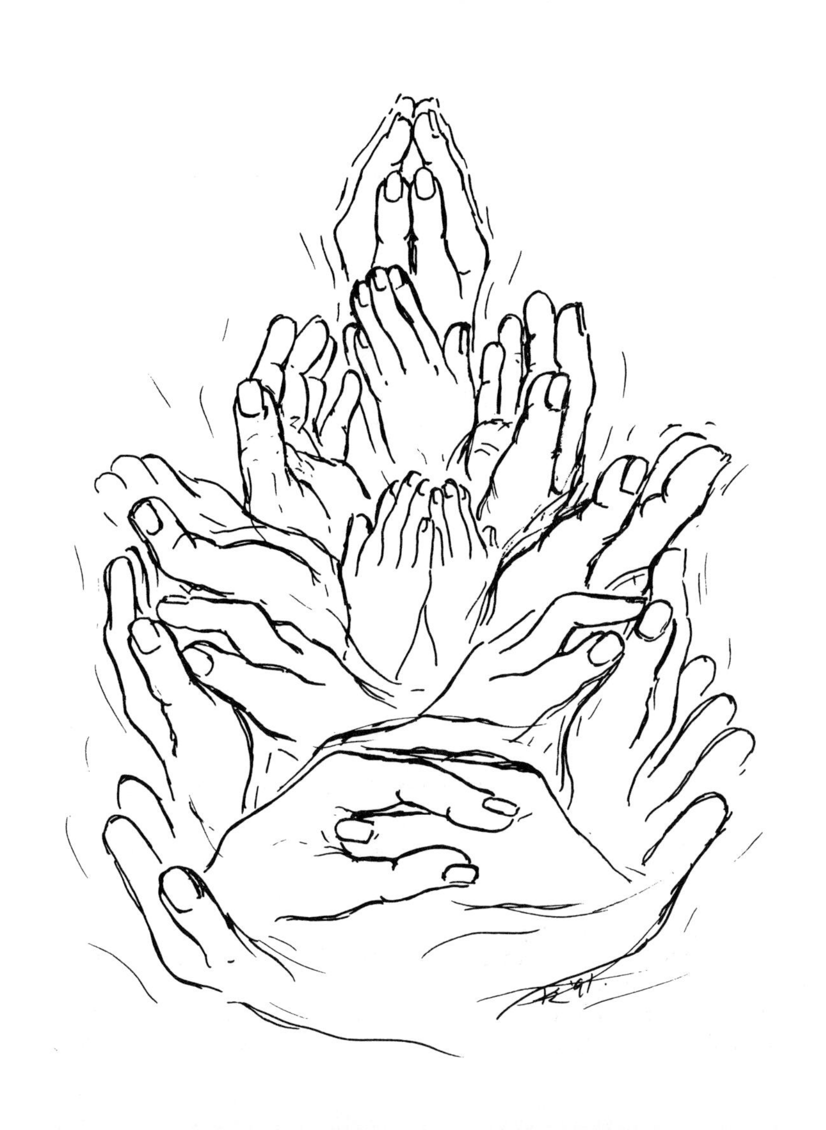

Part Three: FOLLOWING THROUGH

Chapter 1
OUT INTO THE WORLD

We never really left it, did we?

There are occasions when taking a total break away from the everyday life of the world is a real treat. Finding a place and a space where everything that usually absorbs us can be laid on one side, and we can give all our energies to looking at and listening to things of the spirit, is often spoken of as 'going on retreat'. If our daily stilling becomes our staple bread and butter, and sharing stillness in a group is like a family dinner, then taking a retreat is akin to the occasional wedding feast. But this book has not been about the occasional wedding feast, and nothing in it involves any sense of 'leaving the world'. So these last few pages are about taking what we have found in the silence back into the world, although in fact we never left it.

People who regularly practise stillness find two things above all: firstly, they discover — quite surprisingly — that it is absolutely essential to their everyday living, just as much as their daily diet. Silence is something upon which they depend and without which they feel undernourished and lost. Secondly, they discover — also gradually and surprisingly — that the sense of 'anchoredness' spreads under whatever they are doing in everyday living: all the threats and disturbances, all the rows and the challenges, all the delights and the sharings, are soaked with the seeping knowledge that *in the end* all will be well. It's rather like being fed from the roots upwards. No special flags to fly or achievements to flaunt, just a knowing and a certain well-being. If their 'being' is well, that will affect their 'doings' as a sense of proportion and a sort of balance comes through from below ground. In a very practical way, all that is needed before a tricky event of any sort, or during a difficult personal incident, is a quick dip, an instant split-second dive, into the familiar source of centre where stability is an experienced reality.

Not that people who are in the habit of centering are protected from evil. Some have the experience of being set on the front line of attacks from evil, perhaps just because they are close to the heart of God. But all those who want to want to centre[1] and affect the ultimate plan for our world surely want to want to affirm the good and weaken the evil. It is becoming increasingly apparent that simply to ignore evil is not enough; any woolly idea that if we don't look at evil it will get bored and go away, is wildly inadequate. Strong forces can only be disarmed by strong forces.

Perhaps this is a crunch question: is it precisely because in the world of today there is a void where there used to be a persistent affirmation of the presentness of the Creator that disasters and dismays on a grand scale are managing to put in such a strong act? Does the absence of acclamation create a vacuum into which the forces of evil can rush and fill? Historically speaking, this neglect of a constant affirmation of good may be due to modern apathy or indifference or ignorance or overemphasis on petition/penitence. Whatever causes the hole, if more people simply assented to the being of God rather more wholeheartedly, would the void be weakened? If that is the case, then it really is true that we can all, *all*, play a part in the eventual overthrow of evil. It would mean that everyone, *everyone*, bears some responsibility in this astonishing cosmic drama.

There is huge urgency in the message: we *all must get in touch* with our deepest source of *other*. One of the confusing paradoxes in this is that the tools we have to use to combat evil are to do with words like quiet and calm and stillness and patience and peace: yet our human impatience cries out for things made up of forceful imperatives that are as obvious and impelling as the evil forces we are facing. We have to resist using the ploys the enemy uses, even though they seem to bring strength. Instead, we have to use the seepage techniques of private centering as well as, at times, the peaking techniques of public proclaiming and acting.

There is a rich array of phrases used by recognized teachers to describe the act of centering. For instance, Thomas Merton describes it simply as: 'Going to one's centre, and passing through it to the centre of God.'

Basil Pennington tells us to:

> 'Simply use the word to go for a moment to the centre and touch ground — to be renewed by the ever present Creative Love.'
> 'To get in touch with what is — just being.'
> 'To take possession of our very oneness with the Son of God . . .'
> 'Gather together the mind that is scattered abroad: from forgetfulness to singleness, from plurality (and disguise) to simplicity and nakedness . . .'

He defines centering as:

> An affirmation, a recognition, a confirmation, of what actually is. Not by word of mouth or thought or even understanding, but by *being*.

Maria Boulding says that:

> God is creating you NOW. He is breathing his creative love upon your chaos, and speaking his word 'Let there be You' NOW; not only once upon a time when he loved you into existence. His creative love bears upon you TODAY.

Gerard Hughes urges us to:

> Try to stand before God and let him know us, not much preoccupied with particular thoughts but just loving . . . You know you are an undeserving beggar, that you have not a leg to stand on; yet somehow it is good to be there, because *it is real*.

And in an unpublished article Laurence Freeman puts it like this:

> As we centre, we become aware of wave after wave of divine benevolence, if of ourselves we possess nothing. All is gift. Letting go the attempt to control, to possess, to create reality, brings the ultimate perception of giftedness.

He continues, that as we learn to share our emptedness, and learn thereby that all is gift, so too can we share our giftedness. And this is a deep mystery.[2]

It was said to me recently:

> It seems as though nowadays we are encouraged to put all our energies into working for a world of *non-mystery!* Of course we must find out as much as we can, but there comes a point at which we have to acknowledge that beyond and encompassing all our flaunted knowing is a world of non-knowledge; a world of wonder and amazement and marvel. In itself this a fund of creativity and joy; so why are we so neglectful of this awe-inspiring, overwhelming *mysterium tremendum*?

Dame Julian expresses the great relief that it was never intended we should carry the responsibility of understanding everything: she says we were never given 'the whit' to do so, therefore it is merely impertinence to imagine we have it. We are increasing our burdens, and underlining our foolishness, if we think that the universe is sufficiently limited to be comprehended fully by humans. She continues:

> And I saw a marvellous high privity hid in God, which privity [deep secret] he shall openly make known to us in Heaven: in which knowing we shall verily and endlessly join in our Lord God.[3]

The prayer given to us by Jesus Christ himself, in its original form, is written in the continuing present:[4]

Our Father, you are in heaven,
Your name is being hallowed;
Your will is being done, in earth as it is being done in
Heaven . . .
You are giving us our daily bread,
You are leading us away from temptation, and delivering us from
evil . . .

It is only by returning to this sense of now,
by experiencing, reclaiming, acclaiming, proclaiming,
the present sense of the Is-ness of God, and the mystery of
the presence of his benificence in this world;
it is only by this constant and continual being in touch,
that we can regain the power of seeing with discernment,
that we can attempt to clear the intensity of other present-moment
enthusiasms which are diversions and distractions, and
that we can bear any hope of coming to right conclusions about
our actions.

So, every day, every moment, as we go into the world and face its demands and alarms, we can take with us
the assurance of the goodness of God,
the certain knowledge that goodwill can result even from evil, and
the sureness of knowing that things of the Spirit are solid.
In taking this solid conviction into every situation, however busy,
however noisy, however foul, however despairing;
in not running away in order to remain peaceful, detached, and
ordered;
in taking this solid core of hope, love, forgiveness, to wherever life
is going on going on,
we find we certainly aren't on our own, and, incredibly, we are
actually taking a part in the epic working out of God's story for
our world.

So it is no peep in and run out, or taste it and drop it, sort of experience, as if it were a visit to a health farm or a trip to some sort of spiritual cafeteria; it is more like the experience of falling in love and becoming hooked, determined to stay rooted in a particular relationship for good. Or like uncovering a well that has lain hidden and unrecognized deep within us, and which mysteriously turns out to be a source of refreshment and creativity that is fathomless. And, amazingly, that's where we started out in Section One, Chapter 1 as where we wanted to get, and what we wanted to find. The more we *know* the well is there, the more familiar we become in getting access to it, the better we are able to use our activity and noise to the betterment of ourselves and our fellows. And play with delight while we are at it. At the Creation, Wisdom was at the side of the Creator,

his darling and delight,
playing in his presence continually,
playing over his whole world . . .
when he made earth's foundations firm . . .
whoever fails to find me deprives himself . . .
happy are those who keep to my ways.[5]

NOTES

[1]Michael Ramsey's repeated phrase — 'just to want to want to want . . .'
[2]All these are repeated themes, returning constantly throughout the authors' works. For specific titles, see the Bibliography.
[3]Julian of Norwich, *Revelations*, ch. 27.
[4]Ascribed to Cardinal Newman.
[5]Proverbs 8:30–1, 29, 36, 32 (*REB*).

Chapter 2
STILLNESS AND LABELS

The English language is marvellously metaphoric. When we want to express the state of being spent, used up, fragmented, we say 'I feel shattered'; and when we want to express admiration for someone who is coping, competent, collected, we say 'He's such a togethered person'.

The need for becoming centered, connected, tethered is perhaps greater today than ever before because our distractions are greater than ever before. In his best-selling novel about the life journey of a motorcycle mechanic[1] Robert Pirsig describes our present situation like this: 'the present bad quality, the chaotic, disconnected spirit of the twentieth century is created by the overwhelming presence of irrational elements crying out for assimilation'; our current modes of rationality are not moving society forward into a better world. For huge masses of people basic physical needs are no longer overwhelming, and so 'the whole structure of reason is no longer adequate. It begins to be seen for what it really is — emotionally hollow, aesthetically meaningless and spiritually empty'. Later on in the journey the author continues,

> I like the idea of 'gumption'. I like it because it describes exactly what happens to someone who connects with Quality. He gets filled with gumption. A person filled with gumption doesn't sit around dissipating and stewing about things. He's at the front of the train of his own awareness, watching to see what's up the track and meeting it when it comes. That's gumption. The gumption-filling process occurs when one is quiet long enough to see and hear and feel the real universe, not just one's own stale opinions about it. But nothing exotic. That's why I like the word.

All the time our energies are being pulled at from every direction and so our attention is being spread very thinly. We envy someone who can hold all the bits and pieces of their lives — all the hurries and the horrors and the hurrays — gathered into one whole, into one deep conviction that in the end all will be well. Such people carry inside them an assurance and a confidence that we respect. This air of unflappability, of equanimity, is not limited to any one type of person: nuns who are Catholic, monks who are Buddhist, farmers who are agnostic, practising Quakers, regular meditators, or ordinary friends and relations — all and any sort of person may have this particular kind of serenity, this sense of being 'gathered', 'togethered', that the rest of us envy.

Labels seem so inappropriate, but we do cling to them. Stillness at the centre may be experienced by those who practice Buddhist spirituality, Jewish Hitbodedut, Quaker silence, Transcendental techniques of emptying, Zen, Yoga, personal hypnotherapy, or Christian meditation. Each practice claims very specific routes and doctrines, but there is a degree of common ground between them. The use of silence as a means of getting in touch with the 'deeps' in our lives has been recognized from the beginning of history: there are tablets of hieroglyphics describing the use of silence which belong to the early Persian empire, centuries before the birth of Christ. Whether we refer to this practice today as one of stilling, or centering, or mindfulness, or meditating, or contemplating, the end goal is to reach for a state of collectedness from which life takes on more meaning and greater abundance. The means of reaching that centre vary in detail, and it can be puzzling to find the way among so many convinced and convincing teachers.

As humans we are all limited. We try to make ourselves feel 'safe' and in the 'right' by making borders around ourselves. Although in general we need these frameworks of definitions for our daily living, there are moments when we feel we are touching something that is totally Infinite, which is unaffected by our puny efforts to tame it, our attempts to put it inside a frame so it is easier to carry around and feel confident about. Sometimes it feels as though it is a terrible impertinence even to try to put a name to it – any name makes boundaries and is limiting. But the name that has lasted in the mind of mankind for the longest period of all comes from one of the earliest revelations of God: it is simply

.... 'I AM'....

It is a direct statement of *is-ness*; that that infinite Creator simply, unequivocally, *is*.[2]

In today's world, where many common terms which try to describe things about God have become overworked, and meanings are loaded with misunderstandings and hang-ups from the past, it is said that 'Christianity is almost impossible for most people to imagine'.[3] God is too great to be contained within church buildings, and his working spreads over and beyond the churches, so that more often than not it goes unnamed. In a recent survey ordinary people were asked about things they had experienced that they recognized as 'religious'; no less than 81 per cent of those who answered said they had had a significant religious experience which changed their lives. They also claimed that much of this experience couldn't be fitted into words. Indeed, 'some of the most valuable experiences we have are the very ones we find hardest to put into words'.[4] Such things may be described as moments of great joy, a feeling of being part of a mysterious whole, and of being in touch with a meaning and purpose to life, but there is a common exasperation in finding appropriate terms to use to try to contain such powerful experiences. So in fact, in our culture, they usually get left untold.

Some have simply called these deeps 'the place of no words'.

In very real terms, the Godhead who is the originator of the universe has also put himself in the risky position of being an option. Just as any parent knows an intense longing for the welfare of their children, and yet knows also the pain of deliberately holding back – when appropriate – so that their children can make their own choices; in a similar way we can begin to guess at the restraint belonging to the Father of all who doesn't bounce into our lives with easy solutions. These experiences hold faint glimmerings of what it must cost the Creator of all that is, seen and unseen, to hold back from *imposing* the kingdom of heaven on what he has created.[5]

The viewfinder through which this book looks at what is essentially indescribable, that which is uncontainable, the *I AM*, is the one brought to us by Jesus Christ. It was he who said and still says, 'I am come that they might have life, and that they might have it more abundantly'. This abundancy for living is poured through that still centre, through that stillness at the centre of all the disturbances of life; that generous abundancy gathers all the scattered fragments together in order that they can work in balance and with power – if only I choose to assent to its action, and to allow time and space for its entry.

By becoming centered in Christ, my scattered personality can become gathered, my fragmented and bewildered self can become rooted and togethered. But part and parcel of that abundant generosity is that it has been left to me to choose the means.

To hold on and to be held, even while we explore. Our only sure source of direction is our own personal knowledge of the God who *is*.[6] There is a sense of intense involvement between the Creator and the created that is the special characteristic of the word of Christ. Christianity is not a 'religion', it is a *relationship* between the God who made me, and that bit of me that he created in his own image.[7] It is not a manual of do's and don'ts:

It is a call
to be...
to be with...
to be with God!

This notion, that God is with us, comes within a hair's breadth of being preposterous, of being inconceivable. But it is just that hair's breadth that makes all the difference. Once it is crossed, and the unthinkable is given space, everything in life changes. If God has been enfleshed, he is with us even in the muck and the mire, the grime and the gore, and he insists he can reshape it into something that is lastingly worthwhile. He really wants to give us the means of becoming gathered individuals, and through us to channel his benediction to the world. In Austin Farrer's words, God is 'an inexhaustible power for good, and an unfathomable fund of inventiveness and contrivance'.

Those who search for stillness in the companionship of Christ have two massive advantages. It is certainly valid to hold that a still centre can be found without being aligned to Christ, however some techniques attain a silence that is without any value-input, as we saw earlier. But the ancient and tried ways of going into silence *with Christ* and *staying there with him* contain an abundance that is over and above the ordinary.

Firstly, a source of living energy is tapped that can never run dry, a flowing of beneficence and goodwill and wisdom which only the blockages I myself put in the way can limit. And then there is a second thing, which at times is almost more important: it is the certainty that if I meet with something that makes me shudder, Christ himself will be with me to see it through. Although the core of stillness is a place of gathering, sometimes I may not like what is gathered. Silence is a place where layers of disguise are peeled away. There may be some disguises I have been unaware of, particularly if I have been determined to see only those things that are acceptable to me. There may be times in the stillness, when cover-ups and social defences are laid on one side, when things which have been pressed down for a long time take the chance to whelm up. While silence can be a powerful release for inexpressible love and wonder, it can also open up unexpressed pain and hurt, or an unmet sense of sin and helplessness. Often we only manage to look at these things through darkened glasses which ordinarily obscure the real situation. Yet if, in the company of Christ, I can look at these things with less protection and know that my feelings are real to Christ himself, then I will also know that he can sort it out with me, and it will be loosened from me. It will free me to become engrossed in the wholehearted, amazed, even bewildering lostness into God that puts every problem in its place.

The Celtic people were so sure of the presence and goodness of God, that they knew *anything* could be dealt with in his power:

> There he walks in my past;
> He walks in all the dark rooms I pretend are closed,
>   that he may bring light.
> I would invite him into my past. Experience his acceptance.
> Especially I'd show him all I am ashamed of –
>   all I wish to forget –
>   all that still pains and hurts –
>   all the hurt I've caused others:
> Walking there in the places I am afraid of,
>   knowing that he walks with me, he knows, he frees.[8]

At other times we may have a sense of evil that makes us know we are part and parcel of a battle that is eternal, a struggle that is continuing and beyond anything to do with our own small concerns; it is then that we take our part in the grappling that was taken on by Christ himself, in an on-going epic of light triumphing over darkness. It is then that we are made aware in no uncertain terms that the conflict is not yet over, and that there is still a contribution we can make to it. That we are enabled to have a look in on that 'cosmic' struggle, at the side of Christ, is an extraordinary statement. Yet at all times we have with us the certain knowledge that the final outcome has been obtained, and that negative influences will give way to the power, the presence, and the purposes of God.

As Dame Julian put it in the fourteenth century:

> God is our constant ground, in spite of our contrariness.
>
> Our soul is a worshipful city . . . and in the midst of that city sitteth our Lord Jesus, God and Man . . . And this was a singular joy and bliss to me that that I saw him sitting; for the secureness of sitting sheweth endless dwelling.[9]

Accommodation

We, as imperfect, underdeveloped beings,
need to live sheltered by boundaries,
walled . . . in defined spaces. . . .

Each space is different.
Each space has a different window
through which is seen the Light.

The Light is outside: it is *Other*.

Each individual contacts the Light uniquely,
choosing large ↔ small
rooftop ↔ cellar windows

Each individual can use curtains, blinds, bricks, and bars
to block out the Light,
to hide from the Light;
they may also have had blockages imposed upon them.

But
The Light is CONSTANT–
UNDEFINABLE–
UNCONTAINABLE–
IMMEASURABLE–
And unaffected by the fact that we each perceive
it imperfectly, partly, differently; because
that is built-in to the way of our creation.

'There are many dwelling-places in my Father's house.'
(John 14:2, *REB*)

Christ is at the centre; the centre of world events, the centre of me. Today, it has been claimed that 'finding God' has become a growth industry. But ultimately the choice is one that only I can make myself, on one side or the other of the hair's breadth decision: do I or do I not accept that God is Our Father, and that he Is? And with the Father is the Son who taught us to pray, 'Our Father who art'. Those four short words encompass the lot: they can be said in acceptance, adoration, intercession, and petition. Constantly used, they block the entrance of darker powers into the world, our world.

We pray earnestly for 'the kingdom of God'. Different translations of Christ's original words variously describe his meaning as 'the kingdom of God is among you' (*JB*), 'in the midst of you' (*RSV*), 'within you' (*Good News*), and 'inside you' (*J B Phillips*). Does Christ mean that he is, with his kingdom, at the core of each one of us, if only we would acknowledge that fact?

If I decide to take advantage of that amazing option and assent to the Being of God, to vigorously acclaim his Being, I can be with him. I can just stay there, in his presence, his power, his purpose, sopping it up like a dried-out and dessicated sponge gratefully allowing itself to be reflated and reshaped, being in-filled with the unfathomable goodness of God. Indeed, the more often a sponge is put into water, the more quickly it will absorb and regain its full shape;[10] the less often it is put into water the longer it will take to overcome its dryness. Far from being a self-stoking, self-stroking, exercise, the practice of continually reaching for God at the centre results in the love of God spreading out from there — perhaps by means unrecognized by me — to the thirsty world too.

The active practice of silence is not a cop-out;
It is not even an opting-out;
It is a knowing, a being, a be-withing;
a One-ing and a joining.

NOTES

[1]Pirsig, Robert, *Zen and the Art of Motorcycle Maintenance*. London, Corgi Books, 1974 (pp. 110, 296).
[2]John Main, tapes and writings.
[3]Brian Harris, *The Independent*, 27.12.88.
[4]David Hay, *Exploring Inner Space*. London, Mowbray, 1987 (p. 81).
[5]Luke 13:34: 'How often have I longed to gather your children, as a hen gathers her brood under her wings, and you refused. So be it.' (Jerusalem Bible).
[6]Taylor, J. V., *Conversion to the World*, in Ecclestone, Giles, ed., *The Parish Church*. London, Cassels, 1989.
[7]Pennington, M. B., *Centering Prayer*. N. Y., Image Books, 1980.
[8]Derived from Adam, David, *The Edge of Glory*. London, Triangle, 1985.
[9]Julian of Norwich, *Revelations of Divine Love*, trans. Dom Roger Hudleston. London, Burns Oates, 1927.
[10]Hildegard of Bingen, twelfth century, says that God is a wetness, a juicyness, a greening. He wants us to allow him to saturate us; sin is rejecting this moisturing and becoming hard and dried-out. *Illuminations*, ed. M. Fox. N.Y., Bear & Co. Inc., 1985 (p. 32, 65).

BIBLIOGRAPHY

Abhishiktananda, *Prayer*. London, SPCK, 1972.
Adam, David, *The Edge of Glory*. London, Triangle, 1985.
Bailey, Simon, *Still With God*. National Society/Church House Publishing, 1986.
Beesley, Michael, *'Stilling' – a pathway for spiritual learning in the national curriculum*. Salisbury Diocese, 1989.
Benner, David, *Psychotherapy and the Spiritual Quest*. London, Hodder & Stoughton, 1988.
Benson, Herbert, *The Relaxation Response*. London, Collins, 1976.
Bloom, Archbishop Anthony, *Living Prayer*. London, Darton, Longman and Todd, 1966; *School for Prayer*. London, Darton Longman and Todd, 1970.
Boulding, Maria, *The Coming of God*. London, Collins/SPCK, 1982.
Brenner, Avis, *Helping Children Cope with Stress*. Toronto, Lexington Books, 1984.
Bryant, Christopher, *The River Within*. London, Darton, Longman and Todd, 1978; *Journey to the Centre*. London, Darton, Longman and Todd, 1987.
Community of St Clare, *No Time to Pray?* Saint Clare Leaflets 1980.
Craig, Philippa, *Living From Within*. The Grail 1979.
van Dixhoorn, Jan, *Relaxation Therapy in Cardiac Rehabilitation*. Den Haag, Koninklijke Bibliotheek, 1990.
Dodson, Peter, *Toward Contemplation*. Oxford, Fairacres S.L.G., 1977.
Furlong, Monica, *Travelling In*. London, Hodder & Stoughton, 1971; *Merton*. London, Darton, Longman and Todd, 1980.
Gaucher, Guy, *The Spiritual Journey of St Therese of Lisieux*. London, Darton, Longman and Todd, 1987.
Harding, Geoffrey, *Lying Down In Church*. Worthing, Churchman Publishing, 1990.
Hay, David, *Exploring Inner Space*. London, Mowbray, 1987.
Hendricks G. and Roberts, T. B., *The Second Centering Book*. New York, Prentice Hall Press, 1977.
Hodgkinson, Liz, *Smile Therapy*. London, Macdonald & Co Ltd., 1987.
Huggett, Joyce, *Listening to God*. London, Hodder and Stoughton, 1986.
Hughes, Gerard, *God of Surprises*. London, Darton, Longman & Todd, 1985.
Kaplan, Aryeh, *Jewish Meditation*. New York, Schocken Books, 1985.
Kelsey, Martin, *The Other Side of Silence*. London, SPCK, 1987.
Jaegher, Paul de, (ed.) *An Anthology of Mysticism*. Burns & Oates Ltd, 1977.
Johnston, William, *Silent Music*. London, Collins, 1974; *The Inner Eye of Love*. London, Collins, 1978.
Julian of Norwich, *Revelations of Divine Love*, (ed.) Hudleston, Dom Roger. London, Burns Oates, 1927.
Le Shan, Lawrence, *How to Meditate*. Wellingborough, Turnstone Press Ltd, 1983.
Llewelyn, Robert, *A Doorway to Silence*. London, Darton, Longman and Todd, 1986.
Main, John, *Word Into Silence*. London, Darton, Longman and Todd, 1980; *Monastic Prayer and Modern Man*. Montreal, Benedictine Priory, 1983.
Macbeth, Jessica, *Moon over Water*. Wellow, Gateway Books, 1990.
Magdalen, Sister Margaret, *Jesus – Man of Prayer*. London, Hodder & Stoughton, 1987.
McGetrick, Matthew ODC, *Meditation for Modern Men and Women*. Dublin, Dominican Publications, 1983.
McKenty, Neil, *In the Stillness Dancing*. London, Darton, Longman and Todd, 1987.
Matthiessen, Peter, *The Snow Leopard*. Pan Books Ltd, 1980.
de Mello, Tony, *Sadhana*. India, Gujarat Sahitya Prakash, 1980; *Song of the Bird*. India, Gujarat Sahitya Prakash, 1982; *Wellsprings*. India, Gujarat Sahitya Prakash, 1984.
Mother Mary Clare, *Silence and Prayer*. Oxford, Fairacres SLG, 1972. *Prayer and Encountering the Depths*. Oxford, Fairacres SLG, 1973.
Ornish, Dean, *Dr Dean Ornish's Program for Reversing Heart Disease*. New York, Random House, 1990.

Péguy, Charles, *The Holy Innocents and other poems*. The Harvill Press, 1956; *God Speaks*. Pantheon Books, 1943.
Pennington, M. Basil, *Centering Prayer*. New York, Image Books, 1980.
Ramon, Brother, *Deeper Into God*. Basingstoke, Marshall Pickering, 1987.
Ramsey, Michael, *Be Still and Know*. London, Collins, Fount Paperbacks, 1982.
Rinpoche, Dharma-Arya Akong, *Taming the Tiger*. Dzalendara Publishing, 1987.
Robinson, Wendy, *Exploring Silence*. Oxford, Fairacres SLG, 1974.
Runcorn, David, *Space for God*. London, Darton, Longman and Todd, 1990.
Ruth, Elizabeth, *Lamps of Fire*. London, Darton, Longman and Todd, 1985.
Slade, Herbert, *Meeting Schools of Oriental Meditation*. Guildford, Lutterworth, 1973; *Exploration into Contemplative Prayer*. London, Darton, Longman and Todd, 1975.
Smith, Martin, *The Word is Very Near You*. London, Darton, Longman and Todd, 1990.
Storr, Anthony, *Solitude*. London, Fontana Paperbacks, 1989.
van der Post, Laurens, *Jung and the Story of Our Time*. The Hogarth Press, 1976.
Voelcker, Cara, (ed.) *Open Centres*. Chippenham, summer 1986–1991.
Waal, Esther de, *Seeking God*. London, Collins, Fount Paperbacks, 1984; *Living with Contradiction*. London, Collins, Fount Paperbacks, 1989.
Ward, Neville, *The Use of Praying*. London, SCM, 1967.
Wallace, Joe Macdonald, *Stress*. The Crowood Press, 1988.
Williams, Rowan, *The Wound of Knowledge*. London, Darton, Longman and Todd, 1979.
Wilson, Jim, *First Steps in Meditation for Young People*. London, James Clarke & Co. Ltd., 1957.